NEW DIRECTIONS FOR MENTAL HEALTH SERVICES

H. Richard Lamb, *University of Southern California*
EDITOR-IN-CHIEF

Advancing Mental Health and Primary Care Collaboration in the Public Sector

Rupert R. Goetz, David A. Pollack,
David L. Cutler
Oregon Health Sciences University

EDITORS

Number 81, Spring 1999

JOSSEY-BASS PUBLISHERS
San Francisco

ADVANCING MENTAL HEALTH AND PRIMARY CARE COLLABORATION IN THE PUBLIC SECTOR
Rupert R. Goetz, David A. Pollack, David L. Cutler (eds.)
New Directions for Mental Health Services, no. 81
H. Richard Lamb, Editor-in-Chief

Microfilm copies of issues and articles are available in 16mm and 35mm, as well as microfiche in 105mm, through University Microfilms Inc., 300 North Zeeb Road, Ann Arbor, Michigan 48106-1346.

ISSN 0193-9416   ISBN 0-7879-1428-2

NEW DIRECTIONS FOR MENTAL HEALTH SERVICES is part of The Jossey-Bass Psychology Series and is published quarterly by Jossey-Bass Inc., Publishers, 350 Sansome Street, San Francisco, California 94104–1342.

SUBSCRIPTIONS cost $63.00 for individuals and $105.00 for institutions, agencies, and libraries.

EDITORIAL CORRESPONDENCE should be sent to the Editor-in-Chief, H. Richard Lamb, University of Southern California, Department of Psychiatry, Graduate Hall, 1937 Hospital Place, Los Angeles, California 90033-1071.

Cover photograph by Wernher Krutein/PHOTOVAULT © 1990.

Jossey-Bass Web address: www.josseybass.com

Printed in the United States of America on acid-free recycled paper containing 100 percent recovered waste paper, of which at least 20 percent is postconsumer waste.

CONTENTS

EDITORS' NOTES

The integration of mental and physical health concerns, while frequently espoused as a core value of effective health systems, has been difficult to achieve. Never before has there been so much incentive toward integration. In many states, new managed care Medicaid plans have made this mandatory, and the result has been many examples of success not possible in the past. Beyond personal bias and the stigma of mental illness, there are numerous forces that support a continuation of the mind-body duality despite increasing understanding of the inextricable nature of the relationship between mind and brain (Kandel, 1998). This duality is more prominent in public systems of health care than in private. Traditional public health, with its roots in sanitation, infectious diseases, and maternal and perinatal health, has evolved into a safety net for individuals unable to afford other health care. Traditional mental health has evolved from state hospitals to a community mental health system focused primarily on the severe and persistently mentally ill (Egnew, Geary, and Wilson, 1996). In the private sector, collaboration between primary care and specialists (including mental health specialists) has seen less evolutionary separation but still cannot claim systematic integration.

In our generation, both the mental health and physical health systems have had to struggle with ever-rising costs. At the turn of the twentieth century, the introduction of insurance into the patient-physician relationship began to balance the one-sided risk of the patient, who bore both the burden of illness and the burden of payment for medical services. However, this separation soon supported the view that costs were not a relevant part of the medical informed-consent discussion. This view was easy to sustain as more and more parties became involved in health care payment, while providers and patients were able to concentrate on medical care. The steeply rising costs of increasingly effective and technical care were thus easy to ignore until recently. Now managed care principles are often seen as the savior of a health care system on an explosive trajectory to self-destruction.

The strong financial focus of managed care companies has been a contributing factor. Health care costs have leveled off. Coordinated service delivery systems have helped document the cost offsets produced by including mental health coverage in a benefit package. Private patients, in a better position to advocate for themselves and less tolerant of barriers, have found their way between the mental and physical health care systems. Studies clearly document the value of this "integrated" mental health care (Strain and others, 1991; Labott, Preisman, Popovich, and Ianuzzi, 1995).

Now the same forces apply to the public sector. Attention to cost has also become imperative. Managed care principles are generally seen as the way to control public cost. In turn, managed care companies have increasingly become interested in public business. But just as the easy margins obtained by reducing excessively long hospital stays soon evaporated, so too will the easy inefficiencies of a public system trained to bill Medicaid for daily structure and support-type day services that are provided indefinitely when they could be provided by volunteers or consumers or peers. Now the risk is that overzealous cost cutting may destroy essential service systems for the severely disabled. Are the lessons learned in the private managed care sector really easily transferrable to the public mental health?

Managed mental health and primary care cost control in the private sector have relied, in part, on an intact public "safety net" into which patients who exhaust their insurance benefits fall. One of the cost control mechanisms was to focus attention on recruiting patients with only modest care needs as "covered lives." When techniques learned in the private sector are transferred to public systems, this is not an option. It becomes imperative to carefully scrutinize the effect of "management" on the severely and persistently ill, who have formerly fallen out of private care (Simon, Von Korff, and Durham, 1994). Savings from increased efficiencies of truly integrated care can be expected, but the benefits may go well beyond cost containment: a patchwork of marginal safety nets may collectively be in a better position to fulfill their role.

Historically distinct public systems are now forced to seek alliances in the "continuum of care" that many managed care paradigms require, while knowing that cost shifts to other systems, such as criminal justice, will be closely scrutinized. Criminal justice funding may be easier to obtain currently than health care funding, but health care funding is still easier to obtain than social services. This gives rise to the need to delineate health, including mental health, from social service costs. Careful scrutiny of the mental health–primary care interface will be required to make such a "medical" argument for payers (such as legislators) without abrogating the commitment to wraparound and rehabilitative services for traditional public mental health clients and without abandoning the social aspect of the biopsychosocial model.

Integration should be applauded. On the one hand, the nature of the illnesses covered in the public sector requires integration on multiple fronts. Physical health, mental health, chemical dependency treatment, and psychosocial rehabilitation must all be brought together. Multiple areas of "dual diagnosis" have emerged in the discussion. On the other hand, federal, state, and community health care budgets, long complexly interwoven, must be made more flexible if they are to stretch further.

But integration has many faces. For the most part, integration is still a superficial collaboration between two separate domains. But true integration is being attempted with increasing frequency. Driven inexorably by financial constraints, it puts public decision makers on the horns of a dilemma. Managed care technologies generally come from the private sector. If public sector agencies fail to learn these methods, they may not survive (which may mean the end for a mental health system despite its proven record of caring for a state's highest-priority patients). Conversely, the private system is eyed with suspicion by public stakeholders because of its profit orientation and lack of emphasis on chronic, catastrophic, and rehabilitative care. Thus the "privates" must learn to hear public concerns if they are to participate in the transition. Who will need to change, how much, and where?

To address this dilemma, a working understanding of the primary care–mental health interface is necessary for all parties. This book, though written primarily for mental health professionals, attempts to explore the realities of the interfaces as well as the forces for and against integration from both the mental health and physical health sides, pointing to lessons learned and opportunities along the way. If integration is to go beyond a dream, relevance for primary care providers must also be achieved. Thus after an overview of the interface itself, contrasting views are presented. Mental health providers can listen to primary care providers and vice versa; integrated systems are contrasted with carved-out systems. Examples of two particular flashpoints of integration give more detail. Throughout, case examples add depth to the experience, contrasting theoretical approaches or principles with reality as experienced by the authors.

Rupert R. Goetz
David A. Pollack
David L. Cutler
Editors

References

Egnew, R. C., Geary, C., and Wilson, S. M. "Coordinating Physical and Behavioral Healthcare Services for Medicaid Populations: Issues and Implications in Integrated and Carve-Out Systems." *Behavioral Healthcare Tomorrow,* 1996, *5* (5), 67–71.

Kandel, E. R. "A New Intellectual Framework for Psychiatry." *American Journal of Psychiatry,* 1998, *155* (4), 457–469.

Labott, S. M., Preisman, R. C., Popovich J., Jr., and Ianuzzi, M. C. "Health Care Utilization of Somatizing Patients in a Pulmonary Subspecialty Clinic." *Psychosomatics,* 1995, *36* (2), 122–128.

Simon, G. E., Von Korff, M., and Durham, M. L. "Predictors of Outpatient Mental Health Utilization by Primary Care Patients in a Health Maintenance Organization." *American Journal of Psychiatry,* 1994, *151* (6), 908–913.

Strain, J. J., Lyons, J. S., Hammer, J. S., Fahs, M., Lebovits, A., Paddison, P. L., Snyder, S., Strauss, E., Burton, R., Nuber, G., Abernathy, T., Sacks, H., Nordlie, J., and Sacks, C. "Cost Offset from a Psychiatric Consultation—Liaison Intervention with Elderly Hip Fracture Patients." *American Journal of Psychiatry,* 1991, *148* (8), 1044–1049.

RUPERT R. GOETZ, M.D., is adjunct associate professor of psychiatry and associate director of the Public Psychiatry Training Program in the Department of Psychiatry at Oregon Health Sciences University and medical director of the Office of Mental Health Services for the state of Oregon.

DAVID A. POLLACK, M.D., is adjunct associate professor of psychiatry and associate director of the Public Psychiatry Training Program in the Department of Psychiatry at Oregon Health Sciences University.

DAVID L. CUTLER, M.D., is professor of psychiatry and director of the Public Psychiatry Training Program in the Department of Psychiatry at Oregon Health Sciences University.

PART ONE

The Primary Care–Mental Health Interface in the Public Sector

Traditional problems between primary care physicians and psychiatrists have persisted, including inability to understand each other, disrespect, mutual distrust, and competition. Unfortunately, although these two medical specialties, which both use a whole-person approach to the patient, should be pulling together, they are often pulling apart.

Psychiatry and Primary Care: Two Cultures Divided by a Common Cause

Mack Lipkin, Jr.

Primary care is the foundation of the mental health system in the United States, as it accounts for the most patients seen, drugs prescribed, hospital admissions, and cases of mental disorder treated. Regier and others (1993) have described the "de facto" mental health system in the United States, in which 50 percent of persons with one of the thirteen most common defined mental disorders are cared for in the primary care sector and only about 20 percent are cared for in the mental health sector. Thus some two and one-half times as many persons with these thirteen mental disorders obtain care for these disorders in primary care. Add to this the even more common cases of presentations that are somatized, disorders that fail to meet full criteria of the diagnostic classification, and characterological disorders, and it becomes clear that current practice is indeed the de facto mental health system. The public generally prefers to seek care for mental disorders at the office of the primary care physician, at least initially. People may also prefer to avoid the personal and public stigma of seeing a psychiatrist because they experience themselves as sick rather than crazy or disturbed.

Primary care physicians are increasingly, although variably, trained to care for mental disorders and the crises of development and living. As psychiatrists, fewer in number, focus on the sickest patients with difficult mental disorders and as behavioral health care gets carved out and carved up by managed care and medical corporatization, access to psychiatrists is becoming increasingly restricted.

Traditional problems between primary care physicians and psychiatrists have persisted, including inability to understand each other, disrespect, mutual distrust, competition, and shared futility in the changing care system.

NEW DIRECTIONS FOR MENTAL HEALTH SERVICES, no. 81, Spring 1999 © Jossey-Bass Publishers

Unfortunately, while these two medical specialties, both of which use a whole-person approach to the patient, should be pulling together, they are often pulling apart. This is particularly relevant in the public sector, where a series of other factors, such as the different developmental history and focus of the agencies, decreases the common ground. Because readers are assumed to be primarily public mental health professionals, this section will emphasize the primary care provider's view of the cultural aspects that influence the interface. This view "from the other side" presents an opportunity for public mental health providers to better understand the colleagues with whom they will increasingly collaborate.

Primary Care and Psychiatry

Primary care is not a set of problems but a set of approaches and functions. The Institute of Medicine recently defined primary care as "the provision of integrated, accessible health care services by clinicians who are accountable for addressing a large majority of personal health care needs, developing a sustained partnership with patients, and practicing in the context of family and community" (Donaldson, Yordy, Lohr, and Vanselow, 1996). Integrated care by one clinician is the newest feature of this definition. Such care is accessible, first-contact, comprehensive, coordinated, and continuous.

A critical quality of primary care is that it is continuous for several to many years. Mutual adaptation of patient to physician and vice versa over time creates the "sustained partnership" described by the Institute of Medicine. Partnership also requires the ability to negotiate and balance decision making. This sustained partnership is often absent in specialty care, including psychiatry. Although many therapists relate with respect, caring, and commitment over the long term, they less often share power and decision making. Four visits to a psychiatrist are average for an individual patient's episode of illness. Primary care physicians intend to care for the common mental disorders, especially those that present with physical symptoms (including depression, anxiety disorders, somatization, adjustment disorders, normal and abnormal grief reactions, substance abuse, and stress). Primary care physicians, to a greater or lesser extent, use psychotropic drugs, talk therapies, and therapies such as relaxation methods, meditation, and exercise. They treat the large majority of patients with mental disorders and prescribe the large majority of psychotropic drugs.

Primary care is frequently dismissed by specialists with epithets like "LMD" (local medical doctor), "quack," "proletariat doctor," and "hack." Primary care doctors are called second-class, ignorant, and uncaring, and they are categorized as appalling, deficient, and derelict.

Psychiatry is the branch of medicine concerned with diagnosis and treatment of the mental disorders and related conditions. It encounters its share of put-downs: "shrink," "head doctor," "spook." Attitudes about psychiatry range from the respectful and worshipful to the magical and fearful. In most cultures, seeing a psychiatrist is stigmatized. Some cultures deny mental disorders to such an extent they lack words for psychosis or depression (which are common in all major populations studied) or hide these issues in vague concepts like "neurasthenia" and "anomie."

Conditions that patients do not feel are mental disorders, such as somatization, are especially illustrative problems at the interface between psychiatry and primary care. They occur as physical signs or symptoms, so the patients do not seek psychiatric care for them and resent the suggestion they might be having a mental problem. In other situations, somatic symptoms are masked expressions of mental disorders, such as panic disorder and depression. In still others, physical conditions like asthma or hypertension are precipitated or exacerbated or healing is inhibited by psychological considerations including lack of social support, stress, or personality style. Conversely, many medical disorders present as mental problems to psychiatrists, producing conditions where primary care and psychiatry overlap and are more likely to need each other's help.

The experience of mental disorders differs between primary care and psychiatry, and mental health issues present differently to primary care physicians and to psychiatrists. To see a psychiatrist, a patient admits at some level to having a psychiatric problem. Thus mental health providers see persons with a higher level of acceptance. In contrast, patients can see their primary care doctor without acknowledging their problem as psychological. They may be less motivated and less able to consider psychological explanations and treatments and often strenuously reject such interpretations. Psychological problems thus present to primary care wearing the many-colored somatic robes of physical complaints. For example, of all the symptoms associated with depression, they may highlight fatigue, impotence, or sleep change (Katon and others, 1995).

Many phenomena present to primary care doctors that are psychological issues of adjustment or reaction but are not mental disorders. Foremost are life cycle stages—the birth of a child, puberty, adolescence, leaving home, having children, children leaving home, retirement, decline, senescence, and death. Other psychosocial problems in primary care are reactions to common events experienced by the patient as disastrous, such as losing a job, developing a chronic illness, floods, war, or torture. Some are common environmental problems, such as chronic violence, physical danger, or trauma to neighbors. Here primary care is well positioned to intervene early before such issues evolve into dissociation, psychosis, depression, posttraumatic stress disorder, or suicide (Lipkin and Kupka, 1982).

Somatization as a Typical Interface Issue

Somatization is a typical issue that illustrates the problems between the two disciplines. Somatizing patients experience psychological and social problems as physical symptoms and so seek medical care for them (Kaplan, Lipkin, and Gordon, 1988). Because they feel physically ill, they resent psychological explanations for their problems, which they are regularly told are mental. When the symptoms are multiple and severe, these are very high stress, high utilization, and high frustration patients for primary care physicians and for those psychiatrists who do see them.

But somatization is also a normal phenomenon seen in everyday life. Almost everyone exhibits somatization in some way at some time, often in culturally typical ways such as "liver crisis" (crise du foie) in France, heart symptoms in Germany, and abdominal pain (agita) in Italy. Somatization becomes a disorder when it leads the person to seek medical care and when it causes significant morbidity, a disability, or social disruption. For physicians, it is an enormous challenge because the somatizers' symptoms are typical of serious illnesses, and of course they can also get sick and die. Of patients diagnosed with somatization disorder, about 25 percent will eventually turn out to have demonstrable organic pathology in the affected system within three years.

Many disordered somatizers have related personality disorders, primary or secondary depression, or anxiety. Primary care doctors refer these patients to psychiatrists because they have ruled out organic problems, recognize obvious character and psychosocial pathology in the patient, and are frustrated by the patient's illness-related behavior. They find few psychiatrists willing to see them in the first place and fewer who do more than rule out common mental disorders before returning the patient. Some mental health providers get split so that they accuse the primary care doctor of neglecting or failing the patient by not working up the patient's physical complaints. These patients are a good argument for a team approach between mental health and primary care. The goal would be for the primary care physician to provide a "safety net" of medical scrutiny that would ensure that possible medical problems get evaluated to the safe and necessary degree; the mental health provider would provide support, over time reframe the distress as psychological, and help the patient find alternative solutions. When the primary care physician and the psychiatrist are working together, are physically near each other, and talk readily, the burden of these patients is lessened. Somatization further illustrates another aspect of the public primary care–mental health interface: though one of the most common primary care problems, somatization has not been a concern of most public mental health systems. If collaboration is to be achieved, such systems will have to consider supporting primary care colleagues with *their* needs.

Tension in the Relationship

Much tension between the disciplines relates to the perceived inadequacy of primary care treatment of mental disorders and of common psychological problems. Multiple data sets suggest that primary care physicians miss about 33 percent of cases of major depression, over half of substance abuse, and at first pass, 90 percent of panic disorder. When the primary care physician is advised of the results of common psychiatric diagnoses obtained with simple screening devices used in advance of primary care visits, little difference occurs in the outcome of care or even in discussion of the detected problems.

The key to both diagnosis and treatment in care of defined mental disorders and psychological problems is the medical interview and the doctor-patient relationship that results from talk between doctor and patient. The interview accounts for 80 percent of diagnosis, level of compliance, and patient and provider satisfaction (Lipkin, Putnam, and Lazare, 1995). Historic deficiencies have existed in the teaching and monitoring of this core clinical skill in primary care (Novack, Volk, Drossmann, and Lipkin, 1993). Since we now know how and what to teach and teaching is documented to be effective and durable, improving medical education in this area is a high priority for all levels of care.

Studies have suggested that primary care physicians use less medication, sometimes including substandard doses, for less time than psychiatrists do. This is adduced as evidence of inadequate treatment. However, "correct" doses (for example, 150 mg of a tricyclic antidepressant such as imipramine) may not be needed in many cases, especially milder ones. Also, the cases primary care doctors are accused of missing may often be milder ones that do not warrant drug treatment and can be handled with supportive regimens common to primary care.

In parallel, psychiatrists' care for primary care patients is variously criticized. Multiple studies suggest that major side effects of psychiatric hospitalization include increased medication use, invalidism, and time lost from work. Additional critiques have to do with lack of usefulness of mental health system to the primary care doctor or to the patient due to a real or perceived lack of accessibility of psychiatrists. When a person is desperately depressed in the primary care doctor's office but refuses to go to the psychiatric emergency room, the primary care physician wants the psychiatrist to react and be helpful as soon as possible, not at the next available opening. The differing culture in which many primary care physicians handle the medical crises of their patients (such as seeing a patient in the ER) additionally allows opportunity for miscommunication when mental health practitioners are accustomed to seeing crisis patients in their own (often secure) settings.

Access reflects a significant cultural style issue between the two disciplines. Psychiatrists maintain schedules and conditions of care that other patients and other doctors find impractical and so lead to dropping out of treatment or not making the visit. For example, psychiatrists use forty-five minute "hours," do not take many types of insurance, and have surroundings and habits that seem nonmedical (furnished with couches). Private psychiatrists, like all other types of practitioners, often find ways to eliminate from their practices the least attractive cases (such as unkempt, disruptive, or manipulative persons), leaving the primary care doctors to cope with taxing patients alone. This abandons them to the public system, which may again exclude them if they do not fit traditional priorities. Some psychiatrists refuse to see or treat persons who do not meet full criteria for DSM-IV diagnoses because insurance carriers may not reimburse them for subthreshold cases, whether or not the cases are devastating for patient or primary care doctor.

Reconciliation of Primary Care and Psychiatry

Psychiatry and primary care need effective partnerships, not competition; mutual respect, not reciprocal neglect (Lipkin, 1997). The parallel sets of complaints each has about the other highlight real problems on both sides of this critical interface. Primary care doctors, despite the reality that they carry much of the mental health caseload in the nation, do miss cases and often treat them inadequately. Psychiatry as a discipline has failed to create access to care for the unattractive and nonremunerative cases or to face dealing with the mental health of the population in the ambulatory or medical hospital sectors.

Public mental health providers have traditionally focused on severely and persistently mentally ill patients, who are not the patients the primary care physicians struggle with most in their setting. Traditional physician-to-physician relationships are fostered more easily in private sector settings than in public. Public psychiatrists often work as a relatively insulated part of the community mental health team. The case managers are relied on more for interagency and interpractice contacts, thus decreasing the opportunity for the personal relationship between colleagues that allows each partner to understand the other's dilemmas.

Outside of both disciplines, managed and other care plans increasingly attempt to restrict direct access to psychiatrists, direct that care should be done by social workers and psychologists, and limit the number of sessions with psychiatrists to as few as five. Recently, fears that primary care doctors will treat more of psychiatry's bread-and-butter cases in managed care systems and that psychiatrists will be carved out of care and denied access to the mentally ill have widened the divide.

How to improve the recognition and treatment of mental disorders and psychological problems by primary care practitioners has been variously addressed. The American Academy on Physician and Patient has developed a comprehensive approach in which knowledge, skills, and attitudes are taught simultaneously with a learner-centered style and a task orientation. This ensures that the learning can be applied and incorporated into the person of the practitioner and that it will have a higher probability of changing behavior. The model has been shown to be effective and highly satisfying and to change behavior enduringly. Subjects taught have included the medical interview, communication skills, common aspects of psychiatry, somatization, pain, substance abuse, and teaching to teach, and the model has been used effectively with generalists and specialists (Fallowfield, Lipkin, and Hall, 1998).

Reconciliation is needed between the two fields. One way is to diminish the separation between the mental and the physical, what is called mind-body dualism, through mutual participation in training in both behavioral medicine and primary care disciplines, at preclinical and clinical levels. A second technique is to have trainees at several stages of training, not just third-year clerkships, work on the other side of the fence. Of particular promise is having primary care residents do ambulatory consultations with mental health specialists and having psychiatry residents do real primary care training instead of the excessive inpatient medicine now typical.

What is not clear is how the various modern practice mixes of mental health and generalist practitioners will work out with regard to care outcomes and patient acceptability (Paulsen, 1996). Clearly, funders want least-cost practitioners to care for mental disorders, but this is often unpopular with the public. Studies have suggested that when primary care and mental health practitioners are physically in the same area, referrals and outcomes improve, as does satisfaction of patient and practitioner. When selected patients alternate visits between primary care and psychiatry, outcomes improve. When feedback is given concerning performance, when performance is tied to meaningful rewards, and when serious leadership attention is devoted to these issues, outcomes also improve.

In the meantime, there are practical and specific things to do to improve the effectiveness of individual collegial relationships between primary care and psychiatry. They boil down to good relationship skills and meticulous attention to the specifics, cultures, and feelings involved on each side. Some of the things to do are outlined in Table 1.1.

When to Refer to Each Other

In the current climate of change, where public systems are moving to the use of managed care techniques, who is primarily responsible for the patient's care clinically (or fiscally and administratively) becomes a focus of attention. Thus

Table 1.1. Guidelines for Effective Relationships Between Primary Care and Psychiatric Colleagues

Caring for the colleague
Cordial and polite demeanor
Intense and active initial listening
Developing a personal relationship
Taking the time to understand the other's world, preferably by training in or
    spending time in it
Ascertaining the stated and implicit reasons for the contact
Negotiating differences
Agreeing on modes and frequency of contact
Avoiding use of jargon or insider talk
Agreeing on relative roles and responsibilities
Consulting on key decisions
Agreeing on who is to communicate what to whom (patient, family, staff)
Communicating in writing re consultations, discharges
Expressing gratitude for referral or consultation
Returning the favor of referral or consultation

specific guidelines may be helpful as to when to call or involve someone from the complementary discipline (see Table 1.2).

Foremost, referral is warranted when the case would benefit from partnership in the care. For primary care physicians, their ability to refer, their own knowledge and skill levels, and their comfort or discomfort with individual conditions each modify appropriate referral patterns. In general, referral is appropriate when the primary care doctor needs help. For psychiatrists, referral is always warranted when the patient does not have a primary care physician or when they need help with medical evaluation and treatment, especially when the patient may be somatizing.

Conclusion

The dominant mental health system is the primary care health system in all parts of the world, including North America. With the adaptation to managed care in the public sector, the lessons learned from private primary care and mental health collaborations must be even more carefully scrutinized and thoughtfully adapted to those settings. Working through the cultural differences between primary care and mental health is the first step in ensuring collaboration for patients who rely on public systems for accountable, nondiscriminatory, and excellent care.

Table 1.2. Guidelines for Referral Between Psychiatrists and Primary Care Physicians

From Primary Care to Psychiatry

When the case would benefit from partnership in the care
For therapeutically meaningful diagnostic uncertainty (for example, for determining if a patient is psychotic or depressed but not for subtyping of depressions)
When the patient does not get better on a full course of standard therapies
When the case is unduly complicated
When a specialized evaluation (such as psychological testing) is needed
When a specialized treatment (such as antipsychotic medication initiation or desensitization therapy) is needed
When the patient needs psychiatric hospitalization (as when decompensated, psychotic, or suicidal)

From Psychiatry to Primary Care

When the case would benefit from partnership in the care
When the patient does not have a primary care doctor
When the patient needs a medical evaluation to complete the differential
When the patient may have medical complications of the illness or treatment
To evaluate possible drug interactions
When the patient gets medically sick

References

Donaldson, M. S., Yordy, K. D., Lohr, K.N., Vanselow, N. A. (eds). "Primary Care. America's Health in a New Era." Institute of Medicine, National Academy Press, Washington, D.C., 1996, 32–33.

Fallowfield, L., Lipkin, M., Jr., and Hall, A. "Teaching Senior Oncologists Communication Skills: Results from Phase 1 of a Comprehensive Longitudinal Program in the U.K." *Journal of Clinical Oncology*, 1998, *16*, 1961–1968.

Kaplan, C., Lipkin, M., Jr., and Gordon, G. H. "Somatization in Primary Care: Patients with Unexplained and Vexing Medical Complaints." *Journal of General Internal Medicine*, 1988, *3*, 177–190.

Katon, W., Von Korff, M., Lin, E., Walker, E., Simon, G., Bush, T., Robinson, P., and Russo, J. "Collaborative Management to Achieve Treatment Guidelines: Impact on Depression in Primary Care." *Journal of the American Medical Association*, 1995, *273*, 1026–1031.

Lipkin, M., Jr. "Pulling Together or Falling Apart." *Primary Psychiatry*, 1997, *4*, 22–31.

Lipkin, M., Jr., and Kupka, K. (eds). *Psychosocial Factors Affecting Health*. New York: Praeger; 1982.

Lipkin, M., Jr., Putnam, S., and Lazare, A. (eds.). *The Medical Interview: Clinical Care, Education, and Research*. New York: Springer-Verlag, 1995.

Novack, D. H., Volk, G., Drossmann, D. A., and Lipkin, M., Jr. "Medical Interviewing and Interpersonal Skills Teaching in U.S. Medical Schools: Progress, Problems, and Promise." *Journal of the American Medical Association*, 1993, *269*, 2101–2105.

Paulsen, R. H. "Psychiatry and Primary Care as Neighbors: From the Promethean Primary Care Physician to Multidisciplinary Clinic." *International Journal of Psychiatry in Medicine*, 1996, *26*, 113–125.

Regier, D. A., Narrow, W. E., Rae, D. S., Manderscheidt, R. W., Locke, B. Z., and Goodwin, F. K. "The De Facto U.S. Mental and Addictive Disorders Service System." *Archives of General Psychiatry*, 1993, *50*, 85–93.

MACK LIPKIN, JR., M.D., is director of the Division of Primary Care in the Department of Medicine at New York University Medical Center and founding president of the American Academy on Physician and Patient.

Although no comprehensive and generally accepted description of the interface exists, understanding of the differing models of care can set the stage for collaboration. It then becomes important to ensure that partners in this discussion share the same language. Only then can misunderstandings be avoided.

The Primary Care–Mental Health Interface

Rupert R. Goetz

Much has been written about the primary care–mental health interface, where opportunities for confusion are plentiful. It may be helpful to look briefly at the differing practice models that exist in the two areas. Keeping these dissimilarities in mind may make it easier to visualize the public primary care–mental health interface and consider the issues we face in collaborating across it.

Case 1

As a family physician, I saw an average of thirty to forty patients a day. Typically, these were given appointments on a "modified wave" schedule, which meant that two or three patients were given an appointment on the hour and two or three patients were given an appointment on the half hour. This allowed me, using three examination rooms and one nurse, to see multiple patients simultaneously. I would go into the first room and take a brief history before leaving the room to do the same in the next. In the meantime, the first patient would be getting undressed; the third room followed. After having completed my first "cycle" through the rooms, I would return to the first patient for physical examination and then, depending on the complexity of the case, write a prescription or perform a procedure. If the complexity was somewhat greater, I'd return to this room a third time after a procedure tray had been set up, or I might ask the patient to come into my regular office (with desk) where we would discuss more delicate or difficult treatment issues. On an average, I had five to ten minutes per patient. It was up to me to orchestrate the flow over the course of the day so that no patient had to wait too long. Actual appointments varied between five and twenty minutes in length (rarely longer, which would have been highly disruptive).

From a clinical standpoint, I would first screen patients new to me to see whether a medical condition was present that would require immediate hospitalization. If this was the case, they would be referred to the emergency room. (I would then have to make rounds there during my lunch hour or in the evening.) If, however, there was a focused and urgently or immediately treatable condition, this would be handled at the same visit. If the condition was more complex or required follow-up, a return appointment would be suggested. Generally, the exact timing of this was left to the patient, though I made "softer" or "firmer" recommendations. Over time, we would begin dealing with more chronic (but remedial) disorders and ultimately develop an ongoing relationship that was either focused on prevention and education or on management of chronic (but sometimes nonremediable) conditions (or both).

Within this daily practice arrangement and this clinical strategy, in which I developed my understanding of the patient's health (and the health of the patient's family) over time, I developed my relationship to my specialty colleagues. Those that could give me focused advice despite the disruptive nature of my calls (which I placed only when absolutely necessary) were the most cherished; those that sent me back clear responses to my referral questions were next.

Case 2

Several years later, as a practicing psychiatrist, my scheduling and manner of practice were significantly different. Working in a community mental health setting, I was given an hour to see new patients and fifteen minutes for follow-up appointments. Scheduling was handled by the front office, and I specified exactly when I wished to see each patient back. "No shows" were tracked down by their case manager, and alternate appointment times were given. I had a single office and would get my patients personally from the waiting room. If a patient appeared agitated (or possibly even dangerous), I would leave the door open and notify other staff in the clinic to be prepared to call 911.

From a clinical standpoint, when I first saw a new patient, I would focus on developing a comprehensive database at that visit. This meant reviewing the intake materials already filled out and completing a comprehensive psychiatric evaluation interview. It was from this (presumably complete) database that I developed a case formulation with differential diagnosis and a preliminary treatment plan, generally involving only medications. (A preliminary psychosocial treatment plan had already been developed by the case manager before the patient was even sent to me.) If within two or three visits I was not able to develop a relatively comprehensive understanding of the patient's disorder or psychological or social situation, I was uncomfortable and requested additional help from the case manager or other clinical staff, such as the psychologist.

Since many of my patients were severely disabled, I felt lucky if they made it back to the mental health center. It was the exception rather than the rule that they would have an ongoing primary care physician. (Acute medical problems were handled by referral to a local primary care or county health clinic.) As a matter of fact, there being an ongoing relationship with either our dual-diagnosis program or another chemical dependency treatment center frequently seemed the much higher priority. Since my caseload was large (as was the mental health center's), telephone calls were screened by the front office staff and routinely first directed to the case manager. The case manager was also the person who made most ancillary contacts necessary to facilitate patient care. I generally didn't need to use the phone. Interruptions in my schedule were few, since I was being paid at an hourly rate. As an "expensive" psychiatrist, my work was highly protected by the agency. Schedule disruptions were generally prompted by a patient who proved unexpectedly complex or required emergency admission because of suicidal ideations. Rarely did I speak with a primary care physician.

In each role, I considered myself to be providing comprehensive and longitudinal care. Yet what I understood to be "comprehensive" and "longitudinal" differed significantly. As a family physician, "comprehensive" meant that I dealt personally with 95 percent of the disorders I encountered, and "longitudinal" meant that I provided care from prenatal to palliative comfort care. As a psychiatrist, "comprehensive" meant that I provided direct care (or at least medical direction around psychological and social care) for patients with severe disorders; "longitudinal" meant that I attempted to follow the patient over the whole course of their illness. As a result of such inclusionary concepts, each role made it difficult to visualize its limits when seen from within that role. Difficulties were much more easily seen from the outside, yet communicating about these to providers outside my current specialty was likely to engender resistance.

How, then, can we visualize collaborating across such differing practice settings as those I encountered? To bring some manner of organization to the interface, multiple models have been proposed. Some take a systems approach, looking at the prevalence and impact of comorbid disorders and scrutinizing the implications for an integrated health care system (Kim and Flaherty, 1997). Others focus on the collaboration between the providers, distinguishing whether collaborative mental health services are provided from a distance or the same location (Doherty, McDaniel, and Baird, 1996). No comprehensive and generally accepted description of the interface yet exists. This leaves open the possibility that communication falters when "apples" are compared to "oranges" by two well-meaning providers trying to solve an interface problem. They may both be convinced that they are discussing the same issue from the same viewpoint but be surprised to reach only an impasse, not understanding.

No matter which model is chosen, it is useful to remember that at the core of the dilemma stands the patient. Clinical problem solving for the good of the patient remains the core task for both the mental and physical health provider. Engel's Biopsychosocial Model was the predominant one in mental health that allowed providers to focus on comprehensive care. An expansion of this points to the importance of understanding the pragmatic difficulties encountered by the patient (Sadler and Hulgus, 1992). Such pragmatics are particularly relevant when asking public patients (often suffering from severe and persistent mental illness) to navigate without confusion between mental and physical health. Thus as clinicians of differing specialties attempt to collaborate, a pragmatic approach to ensuring a common language that keeps the patient constantly in view is necessary.

Map of Interface Issues

When entering unfamiliar or confusing territory, most of us pragmatically reach for a map. An exact map of the primary care–mental health interface in the public sector would be highly desirable. (The providers from both specialties could look it over together to be sure they were discussing the same issues.) However, no such map exists. Thus a secondary means to ensure a shared focus become important: achieve agreement on the type of problem that is being addressed and then try to solve it.

One map of the type of problems that arise in public mental health and primary care collaborations that I have found useful is derived from a grid developed by crossing two concepts: "type of issue" and "view" (see Table 2.1). First, when scrutinizing a problem, we distinguish clinical from administrative or financial issues (rows). Second, when problem-solving at the interface, we agree whether the problem is being seen primarily from the patient's, the provider's, the agency's, or the system's view (columns). Twelve areas of problem focus (cells) result, demonstrating the number of possible issues that may be buried in problems at the interface. Organizations now trying to develop managed care strategies in the public sector generally seek their own solutions to problems. They arrive at numerous solutions to similar issues, depending on how they choose to frame the issue. Thus the map also graphically illustrates the frequently heard assertion that "if you've seen one managed care system, you've seen one managed care system."

For our purposes, the clinical dimension in this model is defined by who has decision-making authority over day-to-day patient care; administrative elements are those that ultimately boil down to hiring or firing of the providers; financial concerns center around who is responsible for payment. This grid is

Table 2.1. Map of Interface Issues, with Examples of Each View

Type of Problem	Patient's View	Provider's View	Agency's View	System's View
Clinical	How will I be treated?	What can I prescribe?	What are the guidelines for brief therapy?	Is treatment of depression by primary care effective?
Administrative Problem	Whom do I see?	Do I need to ask for permission?	How do I get more prescriber time?	Is shared care leading to increased complaints?
Financial	What will it cost me?	Will I get paid for talking with the family?	Who pays for the lithium levels?	Is there enough money to pay for it all?

then used to analyze a complex problem, decide what the main areas of focus should be, and plan strategic interventions.

Case 3

Prior to the advent of the Oregon Health Plan (OHP), I served in the dual role as director of psychiatric emergency services for the Department of Psychiatry and as director of behavioral medicine for the Department of Family Medicine at Oregon Health Sciences University. In the latter capacity, a variety of services were provided. They centered on teaching but offered the opportunity for integrated mental and physical health care at the family medicine clinic. As the director, I provided joint care, consultation, referral, and independent mental health services within the clinic. For the position to be viable under the fee-for-service paradigm then, it had to be funded as a teaching position. Insurance reimbursement for the services was completely inadequate and made it impossible to recoup even a modest amount of the cost of the services. Unfunded care, absence of preferred provider agreements, and use of nontraditional (and therefore not billable) services all contributed to the dilemma. Now, almost a decade later, the OHP has expanded to provide full mental health coverage for all eligible parties. Also now, several behavioral medicine directors later, it has become possible to negotiate in a meaningful way the development of a self-sustaining position. Arrangements between the mental health organization with which the Department of Psychiatry is affiliated and the fully capitated health care plan with which the Department of Family Medicine is affiliated are making this feasible.

This case describes an agency (column) example that hinged on the identification of the critical nature of the financial (row) arrangements. Since these were the ultimately rate-limiting issues in expanding clearly needed services, their resolution became central. Merely arguing the need for more integrated services (which were clearly needed from the patients' and providers' views) (columns), yielded general consensus but was not sufficient for getting more services actually in place. Using the suggested map, it was not necessary to analyze the problem in detail across all twelve differing dimensions (cells). However, it is critical to be sure that implicit as well as the explicit communication at the interface were focused on the same issue: How could the two collaborating "agencies" agree on how to pay for the required services?

Another example may illustrate the application of the interface map. Discussions frequently center on the various advantages or disadvantages of "integrated" versus "carved-out" mental health care delivery. But definitions of "integrated" and "carved-out" are generally not explicit. Careful scrutiny of many of these discussions demonstrates how difficult it is to avoid comparing apples to oranges: systems that all claim to be integrated, when "mapped" across the clinical, administrative, or financial dimension, prove to be completely different structures.

Using part of our proposed map, Table 2.2 contrasts some elements that may be found in an agency claiming to be "integrated" and one claiming to be

Table 2.2. Agency Example of "Integrated" Versus
"Carved-Out" System Elements

Type of Problem	"Integrated Agency"	"Carved-Out Agency"
Clinical	Mutidisciplinary team	PCP clinics distinct from MH clinics
Administrative	Staff model	Separate mental health and primary care provider agencies
Financial	Common risk pool	Separate risk pools

"carved-out." Clearly, an organization that combines all three characteristics (rows) in one column should be considered integrated or carved-out. However, organizations that share two characteristics from one column while possessing one from the other are also common and can claim at least some degree of integration. However, are they then similar agencies, sharing similar assumptions? The table illustrates that although the appellations "integrated" and "carved-out" provide some useful information on the state of primary care–mental health collaboration, it is not sufficient for a more careful problem analysis. A more detailed analysis will generally be required.

This is also the case when seen through the eyes of the provider. In our interface map, if one were to take the provider's view (column) and again compare "integrated" versus "carved-out" elements, differing views would result. Who really controls the clinical care process? Along the clinical axis, fully integrated care could (at one end of the spectrum) be claimed to exist only where one provider offers both physical and mental health services. This is clearly the case for many primary care providers (Schurman, Kramer, and Mitchell, 1985). The importance of these services is the focus of ongoing scrutiny and training within the primary care and mental health communities (American Academy of Family Physicians, 1995; Goldsmith and Miller, 1997). Examples of mental health providers' also providing primary care are less common but can be found in the advent of primary care psychiatry training, which applies primary care skills, along with the psychiatric, to severely and persistently mentally ill patients. These extremes aside, integrated care generally involves the use of hybrid or shared models of care (Pincus, 1987). The ability to develop these may be one of the opportunities of the current Medicare environment.

Case 4

Oregon had a dilemma: the cost of newer psychiatric medications, both antidepressants and antipsychotics, had escalated for the Office of Medical Assistance Programs (the responsible payer), as it had for everyone else around the country. Utilization management approaches, a familiar part of daily practice on the primary care side, were suggested. However, this was the first time that patients and the consumer movement encountered such strategies on the mental health side. Panic at the thought of not having access to medications that are much easier to remain compliant with than the less expensive alternatives was only natural. An alliance between consumers and drug manufacturers applied political pressure until the proposal was withdrawn. Now a highly complex process, under the leadership of another Department of Human Resources Agency (the Health Resources Commission), is under way to address the use of these expensive medications. Technical advisory panels (from which the consumers and agencies are excluded) are reviewing the scientific basis for the use of both groups of medications. A consumer panel and a medical director panel (representing the mental and physical health plans) will provide input, together with later public testimony. Guidelines on the use of the medications will result, though it is not yet clear whether these will represent best practice, utilization management (such as formulary restrictions or preauthorization), utilization review (monitoring), or a combination of approaches. From the patients' or consumers' viewpoint, it will be critical that clinical treatment decisions (the quality of mental health services) remain clearly in view. Given the huge financial incentives of partnering drug companies, the reliability of information on best practice will require the most careful scrutiny.

This fourth example illustrates that the need to maintain a clear orientation within the complex primary care–mental health interface does not pass the patients by. The consumer movement has achieved much to decrease the stigma of mental illness and give a common voice to individuals who may not be able to advocate for their own cause due to illness. With the advent of managed care and increasingly complex systems, the positions the consumer movement takes at this interface become increasingly delicate. On a political level, emphasis on the so-called severely and persistently mentally ill is a mixed blessing. Such a "medical" focus may help protect parity in funding mental health services for individuals with severe illness. It also helps preserve the necessary role of rehabilitation or wraparound services that run the risk of being seen as lower-priority "social" services by conservative legislators. However, such a stance may also marginalize and stigmatize this highly effective movement when primary care providers, in their push for mental health parity, seek the assistance of mental health programs for people with less severe, though still difficult, mental illnesses. Thus careful distinction of clinical from administrative or financial issues becomes a prerequisite for successful strategic planning even at the consumer level.

References

American Academy of Family Physicians, Commission on Health Care Services. "AAFP White Paper on the Provision of Mental Health Care Services by Family Physicians." *American Family Physician,* 1995, 51 (6), 1405–1412.

Doherty, W. J., McDaniel, S. H., and Baird, M. A. "Five Levels of Primary Care–Behavioral Healthcare Collaboration." *Behavioral Healthcare Tomorrow,* 1996, 5 (5), 25–27.

Engel, G. L. "The Clinical Application of the Biopsychosocial Model." American Journal of Psychiatry, 1980, 137(5), 535–544.

Goldsmith, R. J., and Miller, N. S. "Training of the Resident in Psychiatry and Primary Care: Liaison and Collaboration." *Psychiatric Annals,* 1997, 27 (6), 417–424.

Kim, K., and Flaherty, J. "Integrating Psychiatric Services into Primary Care Settings: A Systems Approach." *Psychiatric Annals,* 1997, 27 (6), 430–435.

Pincus, H. A. "Patient-Oriented Models for Linking Primary Care and Mental Health." *General Hospital Psychiatry,* 1987, 9 (2), 95–101.

Sadler, J. Z., and Hulgus, Y. F. "Clinical Problem Solving and the Biopsychosocial Model." *American Journal of Psychiatry,* 1992, 149 (10), 1315–1323.

Schurman, R. A., Kramer, P. D., and Mitchell, J. B. "The Hidden Mental Health Network." *Archives of General Psychiatry,* 1985, 42 (1), 89–94.

RUPERT R. GOETZ, M.D., is adjunct associate professor of psychiatry and associate director of the Public Psychiatry Training Program in the Department of Psychiatry at Oregon Health Sciences University and medical director of the Office of Mental Health Services for the state of Oregon.

What do we want from primary care physicians to make their care of our patients better and our jobs less difficult? We want reasonable access to primary care services, effective communication, reduction in excessive practice interference, and flexible collaboration.

The Mental Health Provider's View

David A. Pollack

How well primary care and mental health providers communicate and work with each other is absolutely critical to the quality of care for many patients who seek or require services from both components of the system. How does the mental health provider (MHP) view this relationship, and what do MHPs want from their primary care colleagues? In the two examples featured here, the positive or negative outcomes are clearly associated with the effectiveness of the collaboration and the attitudes of the providers. I present several examples providing opportunities for collaboration. The situation in the first example is all too common; in the second, all too rare.

Case 1

A forty-four-year-old woman with schizoaffective disorder characterized by persecutory ideas and a tendency toward excessive irritability when confronted with unpleasant news lives in a group home run by a local mental health center. She also has diabetes for which she occasionally sees her PCP at a nearby health clinic. She usually does not tell the group home manager when she is going to see her PCP, and she manages her own medications, so the staff do not know what nonpsychiatric meds she is taking. She denies any problems other than urinary tract infection symptoms and never tells the PCP about her excessive consumption of soft drinks and other high-sugar foods, and he never asks about her mental health treatment or her living situation. He continues to refill her oral diabetic meds and to occasionally call in antibiotics for her when she develops recurrent bladder infections. He has tried not to confront her with his concerns because she has gotten angry and stormed out of his office on at least three occasions, creating quite a disturbance in the clinic waiting room. One day, when he asks her about her diet, she becomes very angry and accuses him of trying to put her into the hospital. He tells her to not come back to the clinic until she can behave more properly.

Case 2

A thirty-five-year-old man with schizophrenia develops lymphoma and is in treatment with the internist in the local university oncology clinic. The internist contacts the patient's case manager and psychiatrist to set up an appointment to discuss over the phone how to comanage the patient's medical and psychiatric treatment. This patient has been particularly unresponsive to antipsychotic medications and was just getting some benefit from being on clozapine. During the course of chemotherapy for the lymphoma, the patient's white blood cell count drops to 4,000. The psychiatrist is obliged to discontinue the clozapine in order to avoid the possible risk that it may bring the patient's white count down, knowing that if it goes too low, the patient will be unable to receive clozapine again. He informs the internist that the patient's current mental status has become more tenuous and prone to psychotic withdrawal so that the oncology clinic staff will know how to relate to him when he is there for his treatment. They communicate regularly during the remainder of the course of chemotherapy until the patient goes into remission. Once the patient is off the cancer meds, he resumes the clozapine and has a dramatic reduction in his psychotic symptoms. The psychiatrist continues to monitor the patient's white count and sends copies to the internist. The internist calls the psychiatrist once in a while to report on the patient's mental status when in the oncology clinic.

In analyzing Case 1 to see why the communication found in the second is lacking, the interface map suggested in Chapter Two might help identify key areas of resistance or difficulty. Why is there so little communication? Is it a reimbursement (financial) issue, with two agencies competing for the same scarce resources? Or is it a (clinical) problem, with no clear agreement between the PCP and the MHP on the primary treatment focus and how the other provider can help ensure that the necessary care is provided? For this discussion, it is essential to distinguish mental health providers or roles such that we focus primarily on the aspect of care that involves obtaining services from PCPs for psychiatric patients rather than the provision of mental health consultation to PCPs. It is not uncommon for MHPs to be engaged in both types of activity, but later chapters in this book deal more directly with the consultation-liaison issues.

As a provider of psychiatric and other mental health services to persons with severe and persistent mental illness (SPMI), I am particularly aware of the increased risks associated with this population with regard to other health care problems. The same issues apply to other persons with less severe psychiatric conditions, but to a lesser degree (Novack and Goldberg, 1996). The concerns about persons with less severe or even subsyndromal psychiatric problems are, in fact, often a concern of the PCP and a focus of the kinds of consultations discussed in later chapters.

Persons with SPMI are at greater risk of developing comorbid health problems and substance use disorders. Numerous studies support the notion that they are sicker, have more hospitalizations and health care complications, and die younger than the general population (Regier and others, 1988; Wells and others, 1988). They often do not have proper insurance or health coverage. They frequently do not have an established or ongoing PCP to whom they can go when ill, much less for well-care or preventive visits. They often, like other uninsured and unconnected people, use emergency rooms and other acute care services for their basic health care provision. Their communication problems contribute to their being misunderstood or misinterpreted. Their presentation—dirty, disorganized, bizarre, agitated, or otherwise unusual—often leads PCPs to discount, fear, or reject them. They get easily frustrated and have difficulty understanding how to get services ("I couldn't find the clinic" or "I lost my appointment slip") or how to follow the treatment instructions they receive when they are seen ("She told me to take the medicine before meals, but I only eat dinner at the homeless shelter, and they won't let me bring my pills there"). They often fear and avoid medical care to the point of delaying appropriate medical or surgical interventions or denying the need for treatment altogether.

So what do we want from PCPs to make their care of our patients better and our jobs less difficult? There is no simple prescription for what needs to be done, since there are so many different practice situations and such variability in the nature of MHP-PCP relationships, but what follows is a collection of concerns that most MHPs would probably endorse.

Coverage

Our patients need some form of entitlement or health insurance that will allow them to be served by PCPs. A significant proportion of persons with mental health problems, especially those with SPMI, have little or no health insurance, often because of poverty or because they have been unaware or unwilling to go through the process of obtaining it. PCPs, when encountering such patients, should not simply reject them if they don't have coverage or instruct them to go get it but should assist them in finding out where and how to obtain it.

Access to PCPs

It would be best if all mental health patients (like everyone else) could have an ongoing PCP (preferably near where they live) for consistent assessment, treatment, and follow-up for their nonpsychiatric health problems. A single provider or team is preferable to a rotating or random system of providers. The key factors associated with this are attitudes and knowledge. We need PCPs to be interested in and not afraid of persons with mental illness. We want PCPs who will accept our patients and will treat them with dignity and respect. PCPs must understand and be sensitive to some of the basic issues of SPMI conditions, such as schizophrenia and bipolar disorder, but should also be able to recognize the odd or masked presentations of the other physical health problems that occur in these patients. They also need to understand the more common complications of such psychiatric illnesses, including denial, cognitive or attentional difficulties, and comorbid substance use, as well as the common side effects of psychiatric medications, such as tremor, akathisia, and tardive dyskinesia. This basic understanding, obtained from training or ongoing psychiatric consultation supports, will go a long way toward enabling the PCP to relate to and work effectively with mental health patients (Strathdee, 1987; Pollack and Goetz, 1997).

Case 3

A thirty-five-year-old man with schizophrenia is seen at a county health clinic. He has a long history of drinking by himself in his hotel room but does not reveal this information unless asked about it. He does not understand the connection between his alcohol use and the occasional abdominal pain he experiences. His PCP, sensing that alcohol may be involved, gets at the information indirectly by asking how the patient spends his time, eventually asking in a nonjudgmental way how alcohol fits into the patient's life. The patient reluctantly acknowledges his use of alcohol but agrees to have the PCP discuss this problem with the patient's case manager.

Effective Communication

We need to be able to reach PCPs in a reasonable time and fashion, so we can discuss a variety of matters:

- Brief curbside consultations regarding lab results or medical symptoms
- Specific new cases we wish to refer
- Ongoing shared cases with which we need help and advice
- Ongoing shared cases about whom we want specific tests or services
- Cases in which we anticipate behavioral management concerns for the PCP and for which we wish to offer help or advice
- Service authorization approval

The ease with which we can access the PCP (by phone, pager, e-mail, or regular mail) and the receptivity of the PCP to our requests for advice or input are major factors in improving communication. Granted, we need to be sensitive to the pace and pressure PCPs operate under (Cirigliano and Morrison, 1997). We need to conform our requests and advice to be concise and courteous. We must also recognize the limitations of knowledge and skills of some of our PCP colleagues. We can do this by gauging their apparent understanding and interest in our patients. We can only do this, however, if they are willing to reach out to us with questions or concerns about our patients and to communicate spontaneously rather than simply waiting for our calls. They need to respond respectfully to our need for concise clinical explanations of confusing symptoms or unusual lab results, just as they expect us to be to the point in our communications with them about psychiatric concerns. Conversely, mental health providers must also be willing to reciprocate and to be available to respond to the questions and concerns expressed by their primary care colleagues. Methods for doing this are described in a later chapter.

Reduction in Practice Interference

The expression "practice interference" may sound defensive, but it is appropriate: the impact of managed care has led to the need to address how to not intrude when it isn't necessary as well as how to interact and collaborate more effectively. Practice interference can occur in three situations:

1. *When the psychiatric provider wants or needs to offer certain basic medical (nonpsychiatric) services directly to patients.* Some managed care arrangements prevent or impede this activity. For example, a managed care plan's formulary restrictions may prevent the psychiatrist from ordering prescriptions or lab tests for routine or minor nonpsychiatric conditions, even though it might be adequate or more efficient to do so rather than referring the patient, who is primarily served at the community mental health facility, back to the PCP or having to go through a cumbersome and time-consuming request for authorization from the PCP.

2. *When the psychiatric provider or system needs to offer certain psychiatric services for patients.* Some managed care plans restrict psychiatric medications on their formulary, especially newer antidepressants and atypical antipsychotics, as well as drugs that are not used exclusively for psychiatric problems (for example, valproate, clonidine, or beta blockers). They may also restrict the use of certain psychiatric services, such as rehabilitation or outreach, without getting prior approval or authorization. If the gatekeeper for the authorization is the PCP, an awkward and inherently backward situation is set up in which a provider, who may have greater knowledge and expertise, is asking for or trying to convince someone with lesser expertise of the wisdom of the treatment recommendations. At the same time, mental health providers clearly need to be sensitive to and respectful of the costs associated with the services that they provide or order. PCPs and psychiatric providers within the various health plans must create reasonable agreements or protocols to allow for generally accepted treatments without excessive oversight or micromanagement. The story of how the public mental health providers and medical directors of the health plans in Oregon were able to negotiate mechanisms to avoid strict formulary restrictions, cited in Chapter Two, is a good example of how a system can respond to such conflicts or concerns (Pollack and Goetz, 1997).

3. *When the psychiatric provider wishes to obtain nonpsychiatric services for the patient from the PCP or other medical specialist.* These referrals are sometimes viewed with mistrust or suspicion by the PCP who is responsible for authorization of care or referrals. For example, if a patient is referred for a neurological evaluation, the psychiatric provider may feel obligated to jump through unnecessary hoops to get such services, especially if his or her clinical assessment is clear and reasonable.

Willingness to Collaborate in Getting the Patient the Right Treatment

In many cases, the psychiatric provider and the PCP must work together to obtain the best results. These cases, which illustrate the importance of the interface, can be successfully managed only if the two providers agree on clinical issues. Once a common understanding of the patient's treatment needs has been reached, it will be much easier to address financial or administrative problems that may represent additional barriers to care. Personal collaboration is the bedrock of success at the interface in various situations:

1. *Getting patients from the mental health arena to the primary care arena for necessary medical services.* The psychiatric provider may need to warn and secure the cooperation of the PCP to make sure that if they can get the scared and resistant patient to the health clinic, there will be sensitive care and minimal waiting so that the patient won't bolt. Sometimes there may be a need to frame the information in a beneficent way regarding how to get the patient to accept needed treatment.

Case 4

A fifty-five-year-old woman with chronic psychotic illness has developed a severe cellulitis in her left leg. She limps into the mental health clinic but is too delusionally focused on her desire for relief from intrusive demons to communicate about how she developed this condition. The case manager and psychiatrist call the nearby health clinic to arrange for an evaluation of the infection and convince the patient that she needs to go with the case manager to see the PCP in order to have a special evaluation that might make the "demon" problem seem less scary. The PCP is prompted to ask the patient about the demons as part of the physical evaluation.

2. *Getting patients from the primary care arena to the mental health facility for proper and necessary psychiatric services.* Using tact, persuasion, confrontation, leverage, or other strategic interventions that are matched to the patient's apparent psychological capacity and level of engagement are decisions that need to be mutually worked out.

Case 5

A sixty-year-old isolated and fearful woman with schizophrenia has unremitting delusions that she is infected with HIV, in spite of overwhelming observed evidence by her residential manager and mental health team that she does not use IV drugs and is sexually inactive. She persistently comes to the health clinic almost weekly to demand that she be tested for HIV, which the clinic staff have refused to do since she tested negative. The PCP consults with the mental health case manager to devise a plan for getting her to come to the mental health center by offering her free meals and educational sessions on how to prevent AIDS. Once she comes to the mental health center, the treating psychiatrist proposes that she accept antipsychotic medications as a means of dealing with her concern about AIDS, a delusion that gradually subsides as she gets back on her medications.

3. *Getting proper and necessary services to patients when they are unwilling or unable to go to the traditionally appropriate arena.* Identifying effective and palatable incentives for patients to comply with recommended services sometimes requires a great deal of flexibility and creativity.

Case 6

The residents of a residential hotel for formerly homeless mentally ill adults are expected to be skin-tested or to receive chest X-rays annually for tuberculosis-screening purposes. However, a number of the residents fail to comply with the staff's requests, cajoling, and firm guidance to obtain the desired tests. Rather than evicting the uncooperative residents, the staff arrange with the local health clinic to close the hotel for the occasional necessary spraying for roaches and to simultaneously have the mobile X-ray unit just outside the building. They provide the residents with free meal vouchers after they obtain their X-rays.

Conclusion

Psychiatrists and other mental health providers in public sector settings have often been criticized for not attending adequately to the primary care needs of their patients. Unfortunately, this is too often true. It is also true, however, that it has been difficult for PCPs to develop the willingness and ability to work collaboratively with their psychiatric colleagues, especially when the patients in question are suffering from more severe mental health conditions.

If PCPs can endorse and provide the supports described in this chapter—adequate health coverage for persons with psychiatric illnesses, reasonable access to primary care provider services, effective communication, reduction in excessive practice interference, and flexible collaboration in getting the patient the right services—our work together will be much more successful and rewarding for both types of providers and especially for our patients.

References

Cirigliano, M. D., and Morrison, M. "The Primary Care Perspective: Culture and Reality." In J. D. Haber and G. E. Mitchell (eds.), *Primary Care Meets Mental Health.* Tiburon, Calif.: CentraLink Publications, 1997.

Novack, D. H., and Goldberg, R. J. "Psychiatric Problems in Primary Care Patients." *Journal of General Internal Medicine,* 1996, *11,* 56–57.

Pollack, D. A., and Goetz, R. R. "Psychiatric Interface with Primary Care." In K. Minkoff and D. A. Pollack (eds.), *Managed Mental Health Care in the Public Sector: A Survival Manual.* Newark, N.J.: Harwood, 1997.

Regier, D. A., Boyd, J. H., Burke, J. D., Jr., Rae, D. S., Myers, J. K., Kramer, M., Robins, L.N., George, L. K., Karno, M., Locke, B.Z. "One-Month Prevalence of Mental Disorders in the United States: Based on Five Epidemiologic Catchment Area Sites." *Archives of General Psychiatry*, 1988, *45*, 977–986.
Strathdee, G. "Primary Care–Psychiatry Interaction: A British Perspective." *General Hospital Psychiatry*, 1987, *9*, 102–110.
Wells, K. B., Golding, J. M., Burnam, M. A. "Psychiatric Disorders in a Sample of the General Population with and Without Chronic Medical Conditions." *American Journal of Psychiatry*, 1988, *145*, 976–981.

DAVID A. POLLACK, M.D., is adjunct associate professor of psychiatry and associate director of the Public Psychiatry Training Program in the Department of Psychiatry at Oregon Health Sciences University.

To take advantage of the services of mental health professionals,
primary care physicians must improve their flexibility, communication,
and teamwork. All parties must be willing to surrender a measure of
autonomy and control, but the result is worth the effort.

The Primary Care Provider's View

Frank V. deGruy, III

This chapter describes how mental health problems and mental health care appear to the primary care clinician in public practice, how the PCP responds to these problems, and how the primary and mental health care clinicians can work together for the benefit of the patient and the overall system of care.

Case Example

I am scheduled to see sixteen patients in four hours this afternoon; three of them are new patients. I also have to make five patient-related telephone calls. One of the new patients and two of the established patients are also under the care of a clinician at the Community Mental Health Center (CMHC) with whom I have spent five years developing a close collaborative relationship. Half of the patients in my practice are under one of two different managed care contracts, one of which has limited mental health benefits managed by an almost completely inaccessible carve-out company. The mental health of the Medicaid patients in this practice is under the management of the CMHC.

My first patient is here for a Pap smear and mammogram only, and my second patient is a child with an uncomplicated otitis media, so I am on time when I enter the room of my third patient. Beulah Thorncroft is a seventy-five-year-old woman with breast cancer, diabetes mellitus, recent-onset congestive heart failure, hypercholesterolemia, and chronic severe depression. She is currently on six medications, one of which is sertraline, 200 mg per day. She complains of headache, vomiting, and insomnia, which she ascribes to the sertraline, and increasing dyspnea, which she cannot explain. She has previously been unable to tolerate tricyclic antidepressants because of the anticholinergic side effects. She reports that her depression is better, but she can't stand the side effects, which appeared after her last dosage increase. Physical examination suggests worsening congestive heart failure. I send her for a chest X-ray and put in a call to Dr. Mosley, a psychiatrist at the CMHC, who has never seen her. We have a brief conversation. Within thirty minutes, her heart failure medications have been adjusted, her sertraline has been reduced by half, and bupropion has been added to her regimen. She is scheduled for follow-up in one week.

By the time I reach my seventh patient, I am thirty minutes behind. Gerald Hanes is fifty years old, is intensely paranoid, and somatizes. Dr. Brownsill, a psychologist at the CMHC, and I have been sharing responsibility for his care for three years. He comes in about once a month to see one of us and usually has chest or abdominal symptoms. Today he has epigastric pain, which is a new symptom. He had this complaint last week when he saw Dr. Brownsill, who suggested this appointment with me. A careful physical examination revealed no abnormal findings. Since he had a normal endoscopy three months ago, a trial of antacids is prescribed; he is reassured, encouraged to keep his next appointment with Dr. Brownsill in two weeks, and scheduled for follow-up here in a month. I send a copy of my progress note to Dr. Brownsill.

The next five patients come with "routine" primary care problems: Colle's fracture, Type II diabetes mellitus, osteoarthritis, hypertension, asthma, impetigo, urinary tract infection. The mother of the child with impetigo has alcohol on her breath but denies drinking when I ask her about it. The woman with diabetes appears very depressed and apathetic but denies depression when I ask. The woman with hypertension and osteoarthritis consistently "forgets" to take her medications and has poor blood pressure control; I deal with this problem only superficially today but make a note in her chart to address this issue in more detail later. I am back on schedule.

At four o'clock Dodson Crane arrives. Mr. Crane is fifty-five years old and comes in with his sister. He has been referred by an intake nurse at the CMHC, who discovered abnormal laboratory tests on routine blood work. He has chronic undifferentiated schizophrenia and abuses alcohol. Yesterday his liver enzymes were markedly abnormal, he was anemic, and his platelets were low. Today he is tremulous, disoriented, and dehydrated. After a brief consultation with the CMHC medical director, Mr. Dodson is admitted to the hospital, to my service, to deal with his multiple medical problems.

Three more patients to see, five calls to make, and I head for the hospital at six. Not a bad day.

Characteristics of Primary Care Practice

The clinical scenario illustrates several features of primary care practice that have salience for public mental health care and mental health professionals:

1. The pace of practice is fast, visits are short, and many problems are being handled concurrently (deGruy, 1997b, p. 14). Interruptions are frequent and necessary to get the job done.

2. Many primary care patients have behavioral problems, which require a range of responses from the primary care provider and his or her consultants. It is impossible, and probably inappropriate, to deal with all of the identified or suspected behavioral problems as separate diagnostic entities. Behavioral problems are woven into the fabric of primary medical care—to practice primary care is to practice behavioral medicine (deGruy, 1997b, p. 5).

3. Many of the most intractable problems do not fit into the DSM nosology and in fact cannot be construed as mental disorders. Nevertheless, these problems would sometimes yield to the attentions of a dedicated mental health professional.

4. Perhaps five of these patients would qualify for a DSM diagnosis but went unidentified (Spitzer and others, 1994). Likewise, three or four probably have a history of significant sexual or physical abuse (Dickinson, deGruy, Dickinson, and Candib, 1998a, 1998b), and would most likely benefit from identification and intervention. It could also be pointed out that two patients were due for Pap smears and did not get them, nobody was screened for prostate cancer, nobody was screened for glaucoma, two hemoglobin A1c tests "should" have been ordered and were not, and one influenza immunization was overlooked. This list of deficiencies and oversights could be extended almost indefinitely if one wished to make a comprehensive list of all the medical care some group or another has recommended. And this list is in addition to the complaint that brought the patient in the first place! PCPs obviously labor under a condition of competing demands (Klinkman, 1997), and screening for unidentified mental disorders is not necessarily at the top of the list.

5. Some mental health care is rendered out of necessity because the patient will not accept a referral (Olfson, 1991) or will not accept the formulation of the problem in mental terms—this is particularly true of somatizing patients. Mental health care for these patients must be rendered in the primary care setting or not at all.

6. Some mental health care is rendered "invisibly," without an encounter diagnosis and sometimes even without explicit mention in the progress note: insomnia is treated with sedating antidepressants, muscle spasm in the neck or shoulder girdle is treated with benzodiazepine muscle relaxants, and so on. Sometimes this results in suboptimal care, but sometimes it represents an ingenious management strategy that cannot be accomplished in any other way.

Characteristics of the PC-MH Interface

One of the most unusual features of the clinic afternoon described in the case example is the smooth interaction and substantial collaboration between clinicians in the mental health sector and me. This does not happen spontaneously—it takes protracted hard work on both sides.

To take advantage of the services of mental health professionals, PCPs must change in certain ways to improve their flexibility, communication, and teamwork. This is critical to success. However, since the principal audience here is mental health professionals, those issues are not dealt with in detail. This chapter will instead address the issue of how mental health professionals can respond to the constraints and agendas of the primary care setting.

Several key requirements for a successful primary care–mental health care collaboration are illustrated by the clinical scenario. First, immediate access is important. As noted with Beulah Thorncroft, Dr. Mosley was immediately available to offer a two-minute "curbside" consultation that resulted in a rational plan, immediate implementation, and minimal disruption of patient flow. Absent the ability to gain immediate informal consultation, I could have either attempted a revision of her antidepressant regimen by my own lesser expertise or made a referral. This referral would most likely have never been completed and, even if successful, would have prolonged Ms. Thorncroft's suffering for an additional week or two until such time as she had made her way into the MHC system. As illustrated here, the ease of access created a minor disruption in Dr. Mosley's schedule that was justified by the major benefit he conferred. If a more detailed consultation were necessary, it could have been arranged in the near future, at a time when Dr. Mosley or his designee had the requisite time available. This is consistent with the pattern of consultation followed by PCPs with most other consultants and generally results in a high level of satisfaction on all accounts.

Second, medical information must be shared. PCPs and mental health professionals should do whatever it takes to ensure that at least the basic elements of their health care—such as visit logs, problem lists, and medication lists—are available to one another so that efforts are not duplicated, the care of one does not interfere with the care of the other, and they both appear to the patient to be working for the same ends. A common medical record is ideal, but it is likely only if both partners practice under a common managed care plan. Short of that, a policy of information exchange, with patient understanding and agreement, should be part of every care plan.

Third, many of the pressing, important problems with which the PCP deals are neither emergencies nor crises. If the mental health system is structured to respond only to crises, emergencies, and the severely mentally ill, it will be only marginally useful to most PCPs, and the potential for preemptive and preventive work will be lost. The quality of care for complicated mood, anxiety, and somatoform disorders could be improved with even minimal input from an attuned mental health professional. This can be done by a mental health professional functioning as a proactive consultant, reviewing charts or cases, or it can be done in a didactic format with the PCPs as the learners; the consultant-as-educator is an extremely powerful and cost-effective mode of applying expertise to clinical problems.

An extension of this point about the nature of the problems is that much of the difficult and important behavioral work needing attention in this setting has nothing to do with mental disorders at all. Input from mental health professionals on problems such as noncompliance with medications, smoking cessation, violent behavior, and relationship problems could dramatically improve the quality of these patients' lives. This is a full topic in its own right and is mentioned here only as a reminder that mental health professionals are potentially useful against a set of behavioral problems that fall outside the DSM nosology but are nevertheless common, disabling, expensive, and highly salient for the PCP. It is not a topic previously central to public mental health practice but one that offers enormous opportunity for collaboration if realized.

As we begin to explore how best to deploy mental health resources against the mental health problems of a population, or a panel, of patients, it is wise to first take stock of the resources currently being expended in this effort and their distribution. For example, an average of 5 percent of a two thousand–patient panel will complete mental health referrals, and these one hundred patients receive an average of five one-hour mental health visits (Crow, Smith, McNamee, and Piland, 1994): one-fifth with a psychiatrist, one-fifth with a case manager, and three-fifths with a psychologist, psychiatric nurse practitioner, or social worker therapist. This is one hundred hours per year of a psychiatrist, one hundred hours of a case manager, and three hundred hours of therapist availability for this panel of patients. But it is all going to only 5 percent of patients, whereas over 30 percent have significant mental health issues to deal with, and many more than that have significant psychosocial issues affecting their health. Therefore, we may first wish to explore whether there might be a more efficient or effective distribution of these mental health resources. As things now are, the mental health professionals have little choice about who they see and themselves could (and consistently do) think of ways to more effectively deploy their expertise among a primary care panel of patients.

Three brief examples of creative redistribution will serve to make the point. Twelve hours a year of PCP education—a conference a month—might yield more motivated and educated PCPs who would need fewer referrals to make complicated management decisions. Another hour a month reviewing charts of patients with difficult mental health problems might likewise yield improved patient care with less consultation time. Finally, use of a patient educator for development of protocols and patient education materials might yield patients with a greater understanding of how to cope with their circumstances and how to use the system effectively. The point here is that a collaborative look at how we are applying such resources as we already have available usually yields ideas for a more rational distribution of these resources and results in better overall mental health for this panel of patients. This cannot be done without the clinicians from the respective sectors taking the time to sit down together, establishing their common motivations, reaching agreement on a formulation of the problems they share, and inventing new forms in which to apply their collective resources to the better health of their patients.

It should be said here that deep collaboration is easy to call for but difficult to accomplish (deGruy, 1997a). It takes flexibility, willingness for all parties to surrender a measure of autonomy and control, an adjustment in conventions and traditions of practice to fit new models of care, and a commitment to maintain a constant stream of communication. The mental health–primary care interface, particularly in the public sector, has an imperfect fit, for reasons described elsewhere in this volume, and it takes a lot of work and persistence to produce perfect complementarity. But the result—in terms of effective, high-quality patient care—is worth the effort.

Patients with severe and persistent mental illnesses, the main focus in public systems, present a special and extremely important problem and deserve separate comment. Their mental disorder is their defining condition, so to speak, and most of their health care is organized around this condition. This includes such things as assertive case management and psychopharmacotherapeutic consultation services. These resources tend to be located in mental health centers and not in primary care centers. I therefore think it is appropriate to regard the mental health clinician as the primary care practitioner responsible for the overall coordination of these patients' health care. Even if the health care is structured so that a PCP functions as the designated primary, this PCP will not be exercising oversight over the most critical decisions and resources, and it would be appropriate even in these instances to regard the mental health center as these patients' "medical home." This is an important point: the primary care of severely mentally ill patients might best be rendered in the mental health center, with the mental health professional the primary care physician. The family physician or general internist who generally serves as the PCP in such cases functions as a consultant for medical problems, exactly analogous to the role of the mental health professional with "ordinary" primary care patients. His or her responsibilities are to render and coordinate medical care. This is best done from the mental health center, making use of the resources otherwise devoted to each patient's care. The structure of a managed health care plan, the prevailing custom in the community, or the availability of the PCP may dictate that some care be coordinated out of the PCP's office. Either way, an explicit relationship, with clear responsibilities and expectations, can and should be worked out between these two professionals to ensure that medical and mental health care is a seamless whole. This care should measure up to the same standards of availability, communication, efficiency, responsiveness to the priority health issues, and teamwork that I have outlined. PCPs may find themselves called on to function as clinicians, educators, developers of protocols, and consultants for these patients. And just as outlined earlier, the successful assumption of these functions will go a long way toward ensuring that the comprehensive care of patients with severe and persistent mental illnesses reaches unprecedented standards of quality.

References

Crow, M. R., Smith, H. L., McNamee, A. H., and Piland, N. F. "Considerations in Predicting Mental Health Care Use: Implications for Managed Care Plans." *Journal of Mental Health Administration*, 1994, 21, 5–23.

deGruy, F. V. "Coordinating Mental Health Care: What Matters Most?" *General Hospital Psychiatry,* 1997a, *19,* 391–394.

deGruy, F. V. "Mental Healthcare in the Primary Care Setting: A Paradigm Problem." *Families, Systems, and Health,* 1997b, *15,* 3–26.

Dickinson, L. M., deGruy, F. V., Dickinson, W. P., and Candib, L. M. "Complex Posttraumatic Stress Disorder: Evidence from the Primary Care Setting." *General Hospital Psychiatry,* 1998a, *20,* 214–224.

Dickinson, L. M., deGruy, F. V., Dickinson, W. P., and Candib, L. M. "Health-Related Quality of Life and Symptom Profiles of Female Sexual Abuse Survivors." *Archives of Family Medicine,* in press, January 1999.

Klinkman, M. S. "Competing Demands in Psychosocial Care: A Model for the Identification and Treatment of Depressive Disorders in Primary Care." *General Hospital Psychiatry,* 1997, *19,* 98–111.

Olfson, M. "Primary Care Patients Who Refuse Specialized Mental Health Services." *Archives of Internal Medicine,* 1991, *151,* 129–132.

Spitzer, R. L., Williams, J. B., Kroenke, K., Linzer, M., deGruy, F. V., Hahn, S. R., Brody, D. S., and Johnson, J. G. "Utility of a New Procedure for Diagnosing Mental Disorders in Primary Care: The PRIME-MD 1000 Study." *Journal of the American Medical Association,* 1994, *272,* 1749–1756.

FRANK V. DEGRUY, III, M.D., M.S.F.M., is chairman of the Department of Family Practice and Community Medicine at the University of South Alabama.

Truly integrated systems in public sector settings have been few, and most of us are operating in uncharted waters. However, we can embark on this new effort with some eagerness and confidence that collaboration will contribute significantly to the care of our mutual patients.

The Integrated System's View

David A. Pollack

The issues associated with developing an effective mental health consultation relationship with primary care providers in an integrated system of care in the public sector has many similarities with systems in which there is a mental health carve-out. However, there are some significant differences and advantages that must be creatively and opportunistically addressed. This chapter will attempt to highlight what some of these differences are and will describe some methods for maximizing the use and effectiveness of the mental health consultation service.

The integration of a system implies that some or all of the administration, clinical services, and funding are contained within one organization, although the funding may be further divided under two or more organizations' or departments' control (Alter and others, 1997). Since very few such examples have developed in public sector settings, most of us who are involved in these efforts are operating as explorers in uncharted territory (Lambert and Hartley, 1998). Although this is new terrain, we are nonetheless relatively well informed by our previous experiences, either as inpatient consultation-liaison psychiatrists or from operating in large community mental health systems. Both of these background roles require attention to communication and assessment skills, as well as an understanding of what our primary care colleagues seem to need.

Our primary care colleagues need help and advice in managing the primary care needs of persons with severe and persistent mental illness (SPMI), even if their mental health services are being provided in a community mental health program or other specialty resource. Identifying mental health problems as early as possible and providing services in the most appropriate setting, which may often be the patient's primary care clinic, may be the most cost-effective and most satisfying approach for many patients, especially those with less severe psychiatric disorders (Borus and others, 1985).

Primary care providers frequently speak of the many patients they encounter who have significant mental health or substance use problems that complicate, mask, or parade as primary medical problems. They also report that to secure their willingness and understanding to work effectively with the persons who have SPMI, we must be willing to help them assess and treat individuals who have less severe psychiatric conditions. Therefore, we embark on this new effort with some eagerness and confidence that such collaboration will contribute significantly to the care of our mutual patients.

The method employed in describing these approaches will be to use the case example of the consultation that I have been developing within the university-based family medicine clinics in Portland, Oregon. This may be useful in anecdotally identifying some of the issues involved in successfully creating and maintaining such a consultation and by relating the development process for the consultation relationship. Although there are several systems around the country that integrate primary care and mental health (Simon, 1995; Stelovich, 1997), this chapter is intended to describe how to arrive at the fully formed product, not simply to describe what it may look like.

Making the Connection

Public systems have the reputation, which is sometimes accurate, for being mired in bureaucratic and political processes that complicate or obstruct effective collaborations. These public systems, especially as reflected at the state and local governmental administrative levels, often maintain very distinct and impenetrable boundaries between the physical health, mental health, and substance abuse treatment systems.

It is clear that even in health systems that are relatively integrated, such as staff model HMOs or university medical centers, there may be or may have been rather poor relationships or operational integration between the psychiatry or mental health division of the organization and the primary care departments. The main relationships may have been through the inpatient psychiatric consultation-liaison service or through whatever referral system was used to send patients between the two entities on an outpatient or inpatient basis. To develop a more effective and comprehensive consultation relationship, it is necessary to secure the support of the top level of administration in both departments and to recognize that the systems changes may require a gradual and progressive approach.

Case Example

The setting for this example is Oregon Health Sciences University and its hospitals and clinics. This is a large academic medical center that has been struggling to progressively increase its involvement in managed care contractual work. The university's psychiatry department has been relatively slow to develop a more organized practice system for its faculty and resident clinics. It had also developed an unfortunate reputation for being fairly inaccessible to other clinical departments, especially for referrals from the primary care clinics. Some linkages were established through the inpatient psychiatric consultation-liaison service, but only minimal and random connections were operative between psychiatry and the outpatient primary care clinics. The university system is financially integrated but administratively characterized by the separate clinical departments operating somewhat independently.

The consultation in Oregon began with my taking the lead in negotiating with the appropriate leaders within the psychiatry department to cultivate sufficient support to approach the family medicine department about expanding the collaborative relationship. The timing for this proposal was opportune. The relatively new department chair had recognized the need for improved relations with the other clinical departments. He also recognized managed care's impact on the department's financial viability, the growing importance of efficient and effective collaborations between primary care and psychiatry, and the need to cultivate the latter to maintain adequate clinical revenues as well as interdepartmental goodwill. The department chair agreed to provide a sufficient amount of salaried time for me to develop a modest consultation model.

This would involve working on-site in certain family medicine clinics in the traditional role of evaluating, treating, and referring patients who were referred to the psychiatric outpatient clinic from the various primary care clinics. There had previously been a small amount of family medicine–funded time (four hours per week) provided by a psychiatric faculty member to train family medicine residents in evaluating and treating their clinic patients. We incorporated that time into the time being funded by the psychiatry department. Thus the burden of financial viability was eliminated at the very beginning.

The big question was whether the investment would pay off. Would there eventually be sufficient fee-for-service revenues to cover the up-front expense? More important, would we succeed in improving the accessibility and quality of psychiatric services to family medicine such that the model could be expanded to the other primary care departments and clinics? Thus at this first stage, the interest was articulated and a short-term financial arrangement for the start-up was found.

The Consultation Model

To meet the complex service needs of the wide variety of patients with psychiatric disorders who are enrolled in public sector managed care programs, it is necessary to develop flexible models of assessment and treatment. These models must take into account the different locations in which these patients may present and the varying ability that such patients may have to work with mental health providers (MHPs) or primary care providers (PCPs).

Pincus (1987) has eloquently described the various models of managing the primary care–mental health interface and provides a useful vernacular for communicating about the interface. The models vary according to the level of involvement and the types of activities performed by each side. The more collaborative of these models include the service delivery team, the consultation and service model, and the integrated health care team. A recently developed model of systematic collaboration between MHPs and PCPs provides another description of how the interface can be organized to address different levels of patient complexity (Doherty, McDaniel, and Baird, 1997). Strathdee (1987) has identified the attachment-liaison model, which most closely resembles the consultation and service model, as the most effective and popular linkage approach in recent experience in the United Kingdom (see also Creed and Marks, 1989). More recently, Meadows (1998) has described efforts to combine the consultation-liaison attachment approach with shared care for some patients as more effective in meeting the needs of public sector populations, including persons with serious mental illness. Public sector managed care systems in the United States may be most suited to the application of this combined attachment-liaison–shared care model.

For the many patients who surface in primary care settings, it is useful to provide on-site mental health consultation, assessment, and treatment services. This may reduce the stigma and resistance inherent in the referral to an "outside" psychiatric provider. Although this model exists and operates well in some smaller private practice primary care group settings, funding limitations and deficient training of MHPs to act as effective collaborators with PCPs have prevented such consultations from taking hold in the public sector.

The larger the primary care setting, the more feasible it will be to assign a mental health provider or team to work in collaboration with the PCPs. The preferable model would include an on-site mental health professional (available for a reasonable amount of time each week), who could provide consultation and triage services for patients identified by the PCP as having apparent psychiatric problems. This MHP could support the PCP in providing sufficient assessment to determine if the patient required treatment. The mental health treatment could be provided by the PCP, by the on-site MHP, or by referral to an affiliated mental health provider organization. If the on-site consultation is provided by a nonpsychiatrist MHP, it should be augmented by a psychiatrist on-site (probably for less time than the MHP's) for specific psychiatric medical support, didactic presentations, case discussions, and other biopsychosocial consultative activities. The psychiatrist should also be available via phone access, especially for the briefer consultation questions.

The flexibility and variety of services provided through this type of model, including its increased potential for improving and maintaining the mental health skills of PCPs, as well as the improved knowledge of and access to the mental health system for more seriously affected patients, make this a superior approach.

Simon (1995) has described the essential features of such a consultation-liaison model within a staff model HMO. He describes the range of services as including four distinct but overlapping components that require progressively more participation from the MHP and less from the PCP.

The first is the "curbside" consultation, which is usually a brief consultation in person or over the phone, ordinarily focusing on a specific question or problem. The patient is probably not seen by the MHP. The consultation may include certain clinical management suggestions for the PCP to consider and may sometimes lead to a later consultation.

The next level of involvement is the one-time consultation, in which the patient will be seen by the MHP, who serves as an expert consultant and who provides support to the PCP in dealing with a specific diagnostic or management concern.

The third type of liaison service is shared care: brief treatment or intermittent support and joint management (alternating visits between MHP and PCP) of selected cases. This should be reserved for cases that are more likely to respond in a few weeks but may require intermittent follow-up by the MHP. The PCP continues providing the basic health and mental health treatment after the MHP's involvement diminishes.

Finally, there is the option for the case to be transferred to the MHP for specialty care. This should be reserved for the more severe mental disorders. The need for such referral may be readily apparent at the time of assessment or may be a result of incomplete or failed response to treatment provided by the PCP.

Simon asserts that any practice arrangement that hopes to be clinically effective, convenient, and efficient must have this full range of liaison services available from the same consultant (or team of MHPs) and at the PCP's practice site.

Case Example (continued)

With the Simon model in mind, I approached the family medicine clinical director with the notion that he would begin by coming to the three family medicine clinics to "hang out" and see whatever would come his way. He developed a referral mechanism so that residents and staff providers could easily refer patients to him for assessment. He arranged to be present for a number of administrative and educational discussions, including in-service trainings that he presented on topics pertinent to the PC-MH interface.

When not scheduled to see patients in formal assessments, he made himself available to see patients on an ad hoc basis with providers or to discuss patients or other psychiatric clinical issues with providers—in short, to do the curbside consultations that can only happen if the consultant is readily available. He assumed some teaching responsibilities and had family medicine residents assigned to be with him whenever he was at the family medicine clinics. The residents would see patients with him, learning directly how to do psychiatric interviews, mental status exams, and various forms of psychiatric treatment pertinent to primary care practice. When not at the family medicine clinics, he was available by pager to provide curbside consultations to staff or residents at any of the clinics. Thus at the second stage, a consultation model was developed that was compatible with the specific PCP setting.

Access Issues

As one enters into the primary care arena, the question of which patients are appropriate for such a consultation arises. Will the PCPs simply refer any and all patients who have mental health problems, thus inundating the consultant with a high volume of referrals and little opportunity to do the teaching and consultation that would enable the providers to do essential mental health assessment and treatment themselves? Will the PCPs be too busy or otherwise unwilling to adjust to the new resource and therefore avoid making the appropriate referrals? Will the PCPs be able to negotiate the referrals with the patients such that they will be assured that the PCP is not dumping them onto another provider? Can the patients be referred in such a way as to make the process of arranging for them to see the MHP relatively convenient and nonthreatening?

The public sector system tends to attract a higher proportion of patients with more complex or difficult-to-treat problems, especially more persons with substance use, personality disorders, or serious mental disorders, and these factors complicate their primary care presentation and treatment. Integrated systems in the public sector offer the opportunity to identify such cases more effectively and to provide more appropriate treatment for them or, at the least, to make sure that their treatment needs do not go undiscovered. With such complex needs and obstacles to treatment, it is essential to bring a broad array of mental health and substance abuse treatment resources to the primary care setting and to make the access to such off-site specialty services as accessible as possible for those patients who can and should be seen in those settings.

Case Example (continued)

As I began to develop the consultation schedule, I insisted on making myself available to all three clinics, rather than being stationed at the most central one. My intention was to allow patients to be seen at their home clinics. I would also occasionally see a patient briefly with the PCP in order to humanize the consultant and to make the patient more comfortable with the idea of a more thorough assessment from the psychiatrist when it could be scheduled later. I also made myself available for a greater number of hours than had previously been the case so that the potential delay from referral to actual psychiatric assessment could be shortened. The result was relatively swift. Within the first two months, my schedule was full most of the time, with enough leeway to allow for some incidental contact and curbside consultation with the providers in each of the clinics. The bulk of the referrals were of patients who were fairly difficult but whose management could conceivably be handled by the PCP, with appropriate recommendations and support from me.

The early success in obtaining referrals and establishing a mental health presence in the family medicine clinics quickly led to discussions regarding how to expand such services. Within three months, plans were developed to add a master's level mental health clinician, one who was trained in both mental health and substance abuse treatment. This clinician's tasks would be split between the family medicine clinics and the psychiatry outpatient clinic. Direct links to the university's addictions treatment program would also be implemented.

The consultation model was evolving into one that could provide more on-site treatment, including engagement and support services for persons addictions, as well as ease of referral and capacity for service provision in the system's mental health and substance abuse treatment clinics. The new clinician would also augment the services provided by the family medicine clinic's overworked social work staff in facilitating referrals to other mental health and substance abuse providers in the community when such outside referrals were necessary. In this third stage, the context of consultative capacity was adapted to the PCP's needs.

Communication and Collaboration Between PCP and MHP

Confidentiality concerns, addressed in another chapter in this volume, are putatively less problematic within an integrated system. Although one wishes to protect a patient from unnecessary disclosure of personal information, it is essential that the PCP be informed about and able to relate to the content of the patient's psychiatric concerns. The fact that a system is integrated facilitates communication between the MHP and PCP without imposing the burden of obtaining complicated releases of information. This is especially true if the MHP and PCP are employed by the same health organization and have the potential to share records and if the patient has been referred from one to the other.

How to maintain communication is a critical question, both in terms of what should be shared and how to provide it most efficiently and quickly. Major logistical problems affect communication between PCP and MHP. Even if the two providers work for the same organization, especially if it is very large, the mere process of sending or receiving timely messages may be very difficult and can interfere with the provision of services. In the case of the mental health consultation with primary care, a complete report of the consultant's findings and recommendations is essential. The format for such reporting needs to be tailored to fit the PCP, with a reduction in some of the details that most psychiatric evaluations are prone to have. It may also be useful to communicate with the PCP before the "official" note may be available, meaning that telephone or e-mail messages summarizing the MHP's findings may be an appropriate initial response. This prompt response may also assure the PCP that the MHP takes the patient's and provider's needs seriously.

The need to collaborate cannot be overemphasized. However, it is also important to avoid having the communication process encumbered by excessive bureaucratic requirements. Requiring that the MHP and PCP contact each other for every treatment decision or authorization can lead to micromanagement situations and will diminish the value and meaning of their communication.

Case Example (continued)

In my university system, an integrated and automated clinical record has been introduced and is becoming more fully developed and widely used. I learned to use this automated clinical record to dictate and transcribe the reports of my consultation assessments. I would also e-mail the referring provider after each assessment to give a brief summary of the findings and recommendations (or to let the PCP know that the patient failed to show up). This "heads up" note would alert the provider that the more complete assessment report would be forthcoming on the automated record and in hardcopy form to be mailed to the PCP. The report format was organized in a more user-friendly way.

The diagnosis and recommendations were listed close to the beginning of the report, with the pertinent historical and mental status exam findings summarized in the remainder of the report, keeping the report relatively short and to the point. I would also use the automated record system to periodically and systematically review the PCPs' progress notes on patients who had been previously evaluated so as to obtain information regarding clinical outcomes. The fourth stage of the consultation was thus to tailor the consultative communications and follow-up to the PCP setting.

Capitalizing on the Increased Availability

By spending predictable and sustained time on-site, the consultant is able to do much more than simply provide these essential direct services to patients. The ongoing presence of the consultant leads to greater acceptance, by both PCP colleagues and patients, of the role of the mental health professional as a reasonable and legitimate part of the patient's care. This is a subtle but critical factor in increasing PCPs' attention to mental health and chemical dependency issues. The consultant can also be used in a variety of ways to train and facilitate the provision of other useful resources intended to improve the mental health care of the PCPs' patients.

Case Example (continued)

I took it upon myself to provide several unsolicited supports for the family medicine providers. I was able to obtain a charitable grant to provide copies of the new, more user-friendly version of the *DSM IV, Primary Care Version* for all the family medicine residents. I also distributed information about how to obtain psychotropic medications for patients who had no insurance coverage for medications through a comprehensive list of drug manufacturer patient assistance programs. By participating in regularly scheduled conferences at each of the clinics, I was able to contribute the psychiatric perspective on a number of subjects that were presented and discussed and to make presentations on mental health issues. My presence in the preceptor areas of the clinics led to frequent ad hoc discussions of mental health issues, such as specific questions about diagnoses or medications and clarifications about the general mental health system.

In the next phases of the consultation, I intend to introduce more systematic and structured screening and outcomes instruments. As the family medicine providers become more comfortable and experienced in working with their patients' mental health problems, I expect to introduce more streamlined disease management algorithms or treatment modules, especially for depression, anxiety, and somatization disorders. In this phase of the consultation, it becomes possible to address logistical and training needs associated with mental health services more systematically while simultaneously planting the seeds for the expansion and refinement of the consultation service.

How to Fund the Consultation

The issue of cost, which has long prevented this model from being widely used in the public sector, may be mitigated by the shift in payment schemes from fee-for-service to prepaid (for example, case rate or capitation). The inherent value of providing effective consultation as described here (which has usually been a nonreimbursable service) can be more easily justified, since revenues would not be strictly tied to services for which billings are generated. Further justification for its value would depend on acceptable clinical outcomes and demonstrable cost offset.

It is clear that such collaboration will be beneficial to many patients and will lead to decreased medical and indirect costs, beyond the costs that are incurred in the provision of the on-site mental health services. No magic formula has yet been developed to precisely identify how to divide or distribute these costs. The reliance on fee-for-service revenues, if they continue to be available, is unlikely to provide enough income to cover the costs of such a service. The benefits to be derived from the interface work will need to be measured in indirect gains, such as decreased medical utilization and increased patient productivity, as well as ambiguous direct gains, such as increased referrals to the specialty mental health organizations within the integrated system. It is essential to frame this endeavor not as a moneymaking enterprise but as one that improves the goodwill between the primary care and mental health entities and leads to increased quality and more efficient utilization of services in the primary care arena and other areas of the system.

As our example demonstrated, this may require that the psychiatry and primary care departments create a budget for the service based on the staffing needed and the appropriate overhead expenses for incidental costs, especially the costs of communication. The two entities should then agree that they will each shoulder a fair share of the financial burden of the project.

Case Example (conclusion)

The psychiatry department initially provided the bulk of my salary as a consultant. After several months, it was clear that the consultation was critically essential and beneficial and that the service needed to be expanded to include more on-site services, such as the master's level clinician mentioned earlier. The psychiatry department then more confidently approached the family medicine department to request that the latter increase its financial contribution to the service. The negotiations proceeded fairly smoothly, and a reasonable agreement for sharing expenses and allocating revenues was achieved.

Conclusion

We are clearly on the threshold of a new era in psychiatric practice. Care systems are changing rapidly and requiring providers to adjust dramatically to new funding and accountability arrangements. One of the most important adjustments we can make is to improve our collaboration with our primary care colleagues to contribute to their increasing responsibilities for the care and referral of persons with mental health and chemical dependency problems. In integrated systems in the public sector, these collaborations can be challenging and frustrating, but they are achievable.

An important initial task is to get the parties in charge of the separate care departments or systems to accept the need to improve these collaborations. They must also financially support their development by applying the sound business principle of making timely front-end investments for long-term payoffs. One must create or identify a coherent concept of how to structure and develop the consultation. This model should include a multidisciplinary mental health and substance abuse consultation team, tailored to the specific setting or system. This needs to be gradually developed to demonstrate effectiveness and at the same time stimulate demand for service while not overwhelming either the PCPs or the MHPs involved in the process. The use of on-site personnel as the linchpin of the consultation provides a number of advantages, including the opportunity for the provision of independent or shared direct care on-site, as well as training and other resource development.

References

Alter, C. L., Schindler, B. A., Hails, K., Lamdan, R., Shakin Kunkel, E. J., Zager, R. "Funding for Consultation-Liaison Services in Public Sector Managed Care Plans: The Experience of the Consultation Liaison Association of Philadelphia." *Psychosomatics,* 1997, *38,* 93–97.

Borus, J. F., Olendzki, M. C., Kessler, L., Burns, B. J., Brandt, U. C., Broverman, C. A., Henderson, P. R. "The Offset Effect of Mental Health Treatment on Ambulatory Medical Care Utilization and Charges." *Archives of General Psychiatry,* 1985, *42,* 573–580.

Creed, F., and Marks, B. "Liaison Psychiatry in General Practice: A Comparison of the Attachment-Liaison Scheme and Shifted Outpatient Clinic Models." *Journal of the Royal College of General Practitioners,* 1989, *39,* 514–517.

Doherty, W. J., McDaniel, S. H., and Baird, M. A. "Levels of Systematic Collaboration Between Therapists and Other Health Professionals." In J. Haber and G. Mitchell (eds.), *Primary Care Meets Mental Health.* Tiburon, Calif.: CentraLink Publications, 1997.

Lambert, D., and Hartley, D. "Linking Primary Care and Rural Psychiatry: Where Have We Been and Where Are We Going?" *Psychiatric Services,* 1998, *49,* 965–969.

Meadows, G. N. "Establishing a Collaborative Service Model for Primary Mental Health Care." *Medical Journal of Australia,* 1998, *168,* 162–165.

Pincus, H. "Patient-Oriented Models for Linking Primary Care and Mental Health Care." *General Hospital Psychiatry,* 1987, *9,* 95–101.

Simon, G. "Mental Health and Primary Care Liaison in a Staff Model HMO." Presentation at the American Psychiatric Association Meeting, Miami, 1995.

Stelovich, S. "Depression and Its Management in Primary Care: The Harvard Pilgrim Health Care Experience." In J. D. Haber and G. E. Mitchell (eds.), *Primary Care Meets Mental Health.* Tiburon, Calif.: CentraLink Publications, 1997.

Strathdee, G. "Primary Care–Psychiatry Interaction: A British Perspective." *General Hospital Psychiatry,* 1987, *9,* 102–110.

DAVID A. POLLACK, M.D., is adjunct associate professor of psychiatry and associate director of the Public Psychiatry Training Program in the Department of Psychiatry at Oregon Health Sciences University.

Rarely do issues of mental health care in medical settings and the medical care of severely and persistently mentally ill patients treated in public mental health get addressed. The best approach to ensure that care is integrated is to reduce obstacles to reimbursement. In particular, carved-out systems should ask questions that highlight areas for change.

The Carved-Out System's View

Carol L. Alter

Although the imperative to integrate and coordinate care is often cited in the preambles of public sector plans and accrediting guidelines, the majority of such plans do not include specific guidance as to how such care can be coordinated. In fact, rarely, if ever, do plans include mechanisms for patients to receive psychiatric services in any setting but the psychiatric one (Alter and others, 1997). For example, patients admitted to a medical facility, patients receiving care in a primary care setting, or patients with complex medical conditions with concomitant psychiatric comorbidities have no easy means to obtain psychiatric services in those settings.

When behavioral health is "carved out," all requests for behavioral health input are "outside" of the system. While most carved-out models of care take pains to develop "coordination of care" agreements between the medical and mental health providers (MHPs), such agreements tend to focus on the transfer of patient information and pharmacy concerns. Rarely do these agreements address issues related to obtaining mental health treatment for patients within the medical setting (or concomitant with medical illness or treatment). Equally rarely do they cover issues of medical care for severely and persistently mentally ill patients treated in mental health systems. Since the mental health and general medical plans tend to use different panels of providers, this can create significant problems of access, especially when a health care institution or system has no contractual relationship with its affiliated or in-house MHPs.

In the current setting, what financial rationale would a primary care provider (PCP) or general medical plan that carves out mental health possess for providing on-site mental health services? Similarly, why would MHPs invest resources in caring for a population that is similarly "not their own"? Unless there is compelling evidence that providing a greater number or intensity of services will lead to a short-term reduction in costs, extra outlays are often difficult to justify. For the MHP there is a further disincentive, as identifying additional cases in the medical setting can lead to increased demand for services and extra expense.

The best approach to ensure that medical and behavioral health care are integrated is to put mechanisms in place that reduce obstacles to service provision and reimbursement. In particular, public carved-out health systems should ask a series of questions regarding their plans that can help highlight where the system works and where it needs change.

Several issues need to be considered to ensure that care is maximally integrated: Who provides services? (This might be considered on the administrative level of our proposed "map.") How do providers communicate with each other about medical and psychiatric care (the clinical level)? Who pays for services (the financial level)? I will address problems and solutions regarding these aspects of care and care provision in carved-out public systems, using case study examples to illustrate how the components can be identified and included in the development and maintenance of an integrated care system.

The Inpatient Setting

To get a better understanding of obstacles to service provision and financing, it is necessary to apply our questions to the inpatient and outpatient setting separately. Each is sufficiently different that solutions in one may not easily generalize to the other.

Case 1

A patient who has medical coverage from one of three MCOs providing services under a mandated Medicaid managed care plan, BestHealth, is admitted to the hospital's coronary care unit (CCU) for a myocardial infarction. On the second day of admission, the patient experiences confusion and agitation. The CCU team contacts the psychiatric consultant, Dr. Smith, to evaluate the patient. She discovers that the patient has a long history of alcohol abuse that was not revealed to the treatment team and is going through acute alcohol withdrawal. Recommendations for treatment are made, and Dr. Smith returns to visit the patient the next day to ascertain that he has received the appropriate medication and has shown clinical improvement. When the billing manager submits the bills to BestHealth for payment, the MCO informs her that it does not cover psychiatric services and suggests that the bill be submitted to the patient's mental health plan, BestMind. BestMind points out that it doesn't have contracts with the Department of Psychiatry to provide any psychiatric services in that hospital, so it won't be able to pay for the consultation. BestMind acknowledges, however, that it has responsibility for the patient, and if the patient's primary care provider had contacted the office before the consultation (during usual working hours), BestMind would have been more than happy to send out a psychiatric nurse to see the patient. Furthermore, the patient certainly could have seen a mental health professional in the outpatient center.

Who Provides the Care? In this case of psychiatric consultation performed in the inpatient setting, the patient's mental health care was carved out and the mental health plan did not provide service in the same institution as the patient's medical plan. The situation was further complicated by the fact that BestMind states that it would have provided care, but of a different level of service (a nurse rather than a physician), to that patient in that hospital. Dr. Smith was surprised to hear that BestMind's nurse could have completed the consultation, since she knew of no mental health professionals outside of her department holding privileges to practice in her hospital.

To function effectively in the carved-out public system described in Case 1, the provider must fulfill at least three requirements.

1. The provider must have appropriate levels of skill to meet the clinical circumstance. A psychiatrist will usually be needed to assess medical and psychiatric comorbidity, make recommendations for further medical evaluation, and make specific pharmacological recommendations. Although other professionals are very important to the mental health care of medical inpatients, the role of each type of provider must be defined, and never should such individuals practice without appropriate medical and, specifically, psychiatric backup. Nurses and psychologists cannot initiate medical or pharmacological plans without physician support.

2. The provider must be part of the panel. If the provider is not part of the panel, obtaining reimbursement is either impossible or extremely difficult. In many cases, approval may be granted, but only if preauthorization is requested. In the example, that would have been difficult to arrange. This emphasizes the need for community mental health programs typical of the public sector to attend to administrative and financial linkages that before were not as critical.

3. The clinician must also be privileged in the medical system in which the patient receives care. In this particular example, it was discovered that Best-Mind's nurse was not privileged at the hospital. In areas where significant consolidation between hospitals and provider groups has occurred, assumptions are often made regarding the ubiquity of privileging across these new health systems. In public systems, there is often little precedent for MHPs to have contact or privileges in inpatient facilities. Common exceptions are county commitment investigators, who enter facilities to examine patients involuntarily admitted (or to decide on such admissions). While they thus participate heavily in the legal process, they are less frequently considered valuable partners in planning clinical care.

How Do Providers Communicate? This example also illustrates two problems related to communication. First, Dr. Smith learned from the patient that he had a prior history of alcoholism that had been addressed by BestMind. The medical team was not aware of this issue, since none of them had participated in the ongoing care of this individual. As records were shared on a case-by-case basis between the two plans, the patient didn't volunteer his problem, and consent was not obtained to query BestMind's data system and the information was not revealed. Second, while it appears appropriate that the psychiatrist would communicate with the CCU team, the PCP is the only physician who could request a consultation according to the plan guidelines.

Mechanisms that are legal and respect local patient confidentiality statutes need to be established so that patient records of both psychiatric and medical treatment are readily accessible. It has been suggested that patients sign information release waivers on a routine basis or whenever they have contact with either the medical or psychiatric system. In areas where such confidentiality statutes do not exist, a shared medical record or easy access to data between providers is critical (see Chapter Eight).

In a gatekeeper system, consultants need to be educated regarding what can and cannot be done without permission by the gatekeeper. Systems that either carve out specialty care (such as oncology or chronic renal disease) or allow a chronic illness provider to become a "PCP" obviate some of this confusion and diminish the need for some referrals.

Who Will Pay? In this example, it didn't appear that anyone would pay—not a bad deal for either BestHealth or BestMind. But one thing is certain: from now on, Dr. Smith will be less willing to volunteer to see the cardiologist's or the surgeon's patients without first guaranteeing that she was authorized to do so.

Payment optimally needs to be determined as part of the contract with physicians, agencies (including hospitals), and systems. There are numerous models for who pays for these services. In some instances, agreements have been negotiated so that payment depends on whether the patient has primarily a psychiatric or a medical diagnosis. In other instances, the risk is shared based on a formula agreed to by both parties. Particularly in public systems, which bring vastly differing past financial experience to the table, such models must be collaboratively developed and periodically reaffirmed (see Chapter Seven). The scenario described here is not uncommon in the clinical setting. However, it has been the experience of many hospital-based departments of psychiatry that when their inpatient and outpatient psychiatric services are not included in a particular health plan or its affiliated mental health plan, psychiatric services for inpatients may be "carved back in." In this way, psychiatrists who ordinarily provide psychiatric consultation and liaison services are included in the medical panel and can provide those services even if they are reimbursed by the mental health carve-out (Gonzales and Randel, 1996). However, unless explicitly dealt with, other members of a public mental health team may not be so easily included.

Ideally, payment should be easy to get. Psychiatrists seeing patients in this setting perform an average of two interventions. A mental health plan that allows for the initial consultation and at least one follow-up visit without preauthorization avoids significant oversight and authorization expense. Activity based on MHP, patient, and medical attending can be monitored over time so that outliers are identified and overuse is addressed. If this is not possible, subcontracting with the medical providers may provide more efficient and more appropriate utilization reviews, as they have greater capability to review the clinical needs in this setting.

Payment should also follow established rate structures. While psychiatrists in the outpatient setting or inpatient psychiatric setting may negotiate reduced fees for service that may be appropriate or feasible for those settings, the work performed by psychiatrists and other mental health professionals in the medical setting is in fact comparable to the kind of work performed by other consultants (such as cardiologists or endocrinologists) in the medical setting. Fees should be predetermined and based on market rates for other medical consultants.

The Outpatient Setting

Two issues typically arise in the outpatient setting in carved-out public systems. The first involves the availability of psychiatric and mental health input for the routine general medical patient. This is an area of enormous importance to the primary care providers, who seek such help, yet in public systems there is often little prior experience with the type of collaboration they seek. The second involves the special psychosocial needs of patients with chronic medical problems. The public mental health system's experience with psychosocial rehabilitation places it in a wonderful position to offer such help but requires explicit attention to a different population than was formerly emphasized. Here, too, issues of who provides, who pays, and communication predominate.

Case 2

Mrs. Goodbody has had a long history of insulin-dependent diabetes and sees her PCP every three to four months. However, in the past six weeks she has been to the clinic five times. Although her blood sugar has remained stable and within normal limits, she has multiple new "vague" complaints including "nerves," trouble sleeping, poor appetite, and a lack of interest in her usual activities. At the sixth visit, the patient begins to report lack of compliance with her insulin dosing in addition to continuation of the other symptoms. The PCP prescribes fluoxetine, 10 mg per day, and makes an appointment to see the patient in one month. Mrs. Goodbody takes the medication but feels only agitation and discontinues it after five days. She misses her scheduled appointment and five weeks later is admitted to the hospital with dehydration and complications from her diabetes.

Who Provides the Care?   The case involves a patient with psychological distress in the primary care clinic. One important question to ask is what other options were available to either the patient or the physician in this setting. What would have been the financial or clinical impact if on-site psychiatric input had been available or ongoing educational programs aimed at the diagnosis and treatment of psychiatric disorders in the PC setting had been offered? At what point, if any, would referral to the behavioral health team have been appropriate?

The primary care provider must know how to provide behavioral health care services and have time to provide the services or else must have the ability to collaborate with behavioral health care providers and make appropriate referrals to the behavioral health experts.

Studies that have examined the nature of psychiatric evaluation and treatment in the primary care setting by PCPs have found that the ability to diagnose and treat psychiatric disorders accurately is often limited (Brown and Shulberg, 1996; Katon and others, 1992, 1995). However, studies have also shown that when there is ongoing and active psychiatric input, diagnosis and treatment are significantly improved (Katon and others, 1996). This is true not only when the psychiatrist performs the assessment and implements treatment but also if the psychiatrist has an active role in the teaching, supervising, and coaching of primary care givers in the clinical setting.

To adequately evaluate and treat psychiatric disorders requires a specific set of skills. If the PCP is to provide such services, training and ongoing education around these skills must be made available. If the PCP is the mainstay of this care, attention must be paid to the time necessary to provide these types of services. PCPs on a seven-minute visit clock will not be able to determine the etiology or treatment of these complicated problems unless they have been specifically trained to do so (Cole and Raju, 1996).

Alternatively, the PCP can be supported or assisted by other MHPs or can routinely obtain mental health services. As the burden to diagnose and treat the majority of psychiatric disturbances in the primary care setting has increased, there has been renewed interest in having mental health professionals available on-site in primary care settings. Psychologists, nurses, social workers, and psychiatrists have all been used in these programs. On-site availability, however, will function optimally only if there are strong links to the mental health system that can be accessed in an ongoing fashion. Although supplementing usual care with a single mental health professional may improve recognition and treatment, ensuring depth of consultative information and adequate continuity for ongoing psychiatric problems may be limited under these circumstances. In the public sector, such arrangements may be ideal. A mental health professional who functions in both the mental health and primary car setting can support services in the primary care setting while providing a local resource for information on when and how to collaborate in the care of more severely mentally ill patients.

What Is Provided?   In this instance, the PCP followed the patient closely but prescribed no treatment for several weeks and only after her medical condition was affected. Neither he nor the clinic employed screening tools or treatment algorithms to assist in diagnosis or treatment. Several screening tools exist for use in the primary care setting that have been increasingly implemented and have helped to improve diagnosis. The two most widely used instruments, PRIME-MD and SDDS-PC, are patient self-report measures that can be easily scored and will arrive at a psychiatric diagnosis consistent with DSM-IV (Spitzer and others, 1994; Olfson and others, 1995). However, studies have shown that these instruments are not foolproof and may in fact have a high degree of false positivity (Spitzer and others, 1994; Weissman and others, 1995). Further, the Agency for Health Care Policy and Research has issued guidelines for the treatment of depression in the primary care setting (Depression Guideline Panel, 1993), and the American Psychiatric Association has published the DSM IV-PC (Pincus and others, 1995), both of which can be very helpful in improving management of depression in this setting. Although both screening and treatment tools should help PCPs make appropriate diagnostic and treatment decisions, such decisions need to be supported by the availability of ongoing teaching and expert consultation.

The quality of care is dependent on provider skills and knowledge. Providers should be adequately trained in clinical evaluations or in the use of standardized screening instruments. Training should be ongoing and reinforced over time. Treatment decisions should be consistent with acceptable guidelines for dose and duration of treatment. If psychosocial remedies are to be suggested, the provider should understand the implications and effectiveness expected.

Who Pays? Mrs. Goodbody's treatment, whether delivered by her PCP or by a mental health professional in the mental health setting, is certainly part of her benefit. The question is who pays if mental health services are augmented in the primary care setting by any of the methods discussed (on-site psychiatric consultation, other mental health professional presence, or training programs). Cost effectiveness and cost offset studies, as well as studies examining the indirect impact of anxiety and depression, show that the costs of untreated mental illness are staggering, but adequate treatment can have a positive impact on reducing both direct and indirect costs.

Money must be spent wisely. Patients referred to the mental health setting will cost more than treating them early in the primary care setting. The absence of training or on-site support by mental health professionals will lead to poorly diagnosed and poorly treated patients, who will also be dissatisfied with their care. The use of on-site psychiatrists or other mental health professionals can lead to decreased time spent by PCPs on psychiatric, somatoform, and other behavioral health problems.

The financial incentive is thought to reside in the primary care setting. However, MCOs are reluctant to assume these costs. Limited cost-sharing arrangement can be devised so that the mental health MCO pays for patients with a primary psychiatric diagnosis (including all medical care related to psychiatric issues) and the MCO pays for all care related to the primary medical condition. In reality, most public systems' financial responsibility will be mandated by the terms of the state plan as stated in that state's specific regulations or legislation (that is, carved-out or not). If a service is to be provided by the mental health system or by the primary care system, that system is financially responsible. From the state's perspective, it is a continuous system, despite the fragmentation and potential gains and losses attributable to each component.

Specialty Care. Patients with chronic medical illness often have psychiatric and psychosocial difficulties related to that illness that are best treated within that treatment context. This type of care has been provided in the setting of AIDS, oncology, pediatric units, chronic renal failure, and organ transplantation units. There is a wide body of literature documenting the increased psychiatric morbidity for these patients and the benefit to both health-related and psychosocial outcomes with the presence of psychosocial assessment and support. For example, multidisciplinary psychosocial service teams can offer evaluative, supportive, and case management services in concert with intensive medical care. Such services can minimize or alleviate known psychiatric and medical comorbidities.

This type of care is not only clinically important but in some instances has also been legislated, as in the case of the Designated AIDS Treatment Centers in New York State. Each center must provide psychiatric, psychosocial, and case management services, and funding is provided to compensate these programs. These services have helped significantly in ensuring that HIV patients in the state of New York can receive appropriate psychosocial and case management services without having to overcome significant cost and logistical barriers. The argument needs to be made that medically based psychiatric and psychosocial services can and will improve outcomes and are an essential component of case management functions of the treatment team.

Medical Care of Severely and Persistently Mentally Ill Patients. The corollary of providing adequate psychiatric services for medically ill patients is that severely mentally ill patients rarely seek or obtain appropriate medical care. Coordination of care agreements must address this need as well. It could be suggested that such agreements should establish minimum standards of care as well as similar mechanisms for service provision for such patients.

Conclusion

Clinical and research-based evidence suggests that a large proportion of patients receiving care for medical problems also have significant psychiatric symptomatology. The cost in terms of dollars and morbidity of not treating these patients appropriately is staggering. It is particularly staggering when we consider the higher degree of disability that characterizes patients in the public system. Recent initiatives by the Health Care Financing Administration, National Committee for Quality Assurance, and Health Plan Employer Data and Information Set have begun to address the principles of coordination of care. Careful scrutiny of the measures used by these systems is necessary to ensure that they meet the requisite standards of quality in public systems. Public sector efforts, such as those by the National Association of State Mental Health Program Directors' Research Institute (http://www.nasmhpd.org/nri/index.htm), to analyze and coordinate public system outcomes measures must be considered and, where necessary, integrated into such systems. Efforts must specifically address how such care will be delivered, who will deliver it, and how reimbursement is to be structured.

References

Alter, C. L., Schindler, B. A., Hails, K., Lamdan, R., Shakin Kunkel, E. J., Zager, R. "Funding for Consultation-Liaison Services in Public Sector Managed Care Plans: The Experience of the Consultation Liaison Association of Philadelphia." *Psychosomatics*, 1997, *38*, 93–97.

American Psychiatric Association. *Diagnostic and Statistical Manual of Mental Disorders.*(4th ed.) Washington, D.C.: American Psychiatric Association, 1994.

Brown, C., and Shulberg, H. C. "The Efficacy of Psychosocial Treatments in Primary Care: A Review of Randomized Clinical Trials." *General Hospital Psychiatry,* 1996, *17,* 414–424.

Cole, S., and Raju, M. "Overcoming Barriers to Integration of Primary Care and Behavioral Health Care: Focus on Knowledge and Skills." *Behavioral Health Care Tomorrow,* 1996, *5,* 30–35.

Depression Guideline Panel, Agency for Health Care Policy and Research. *Depression in Primary Care,* Vols. 1 and 2. Clinical Practice Guideline no. 5; AHCPR Publication no. 93-0550. Washington, D.C.: U.S. Department of Health and Human Services, 1993.

Gonzales, J. J., and Randel, L. "Consultation-Liaison Psychiatry in the Managed Care Arena." *Psychiatric Clinics of North America,* 1996, *19,* 449–466.

Katon, W., Robinson, P., von Korff, M., Lin, E., Bush, T., Ludman, E., Simon, G., Walker, E. "A Multifaceted Intervention to Improve Treatment of Depression in Primary Care." *Archives of General Psychiatry,* 1996, *53,* 924–932.

Katon, W., von Korff, M., Lin, E., Walker, E., Simon, G. E., Bush, T., Robinson, P., Russo, J. "Collaborative Management to Achieve Treatment Guidelines." *Journal of the American Medical Association,* 1995, *273,* 1026–1081.

Katon, W., von Korff, M., Lin, E., Bush, T., and Ormel, J. "Adequacy and Duration of Antidepressant Treatment in Primary Care." *Medical Care,* 1992, *30,* 67–76.

Olfson, M., Leon, A. C., Broadhead, W. E., Weissman, M. M., Barrett, J. E., Blacklow, R. S., Gilbert, T. T., Higgins, E. S. "The SDDS-PC: A Diagnostic Aid for Multiple Mental Disorders in Primary Care." *Psychopharmacology Bulletin,* 1995, *31,* 415–420.

Pincus, H. A., Vettorello, N. E., McQueen, L. E., First, M., Wise, T. N., Zarin, D., Davis, W. W. "Bridging the Gap Between Psychiatry and Primary Care: The DSM-IV-PC." *Psychosomatics,* 1995, *36,* 328–335.

Spitzer, R. L., Williams, J. B., Kroenke, K. "Utility of a New Procedure for Diagnosing Mental Disorders in Primary Care: 'The Prime-MD 1000 Study.'" *Journal of the American Medical Association,* 1994, *272,* 1749–1756.

Weissman, M. M., Olfson, M., Leon, A. C., Broadhead, W. E., Gilbert, T. T., Higgins, E. S., Barrett, J. E., Blacklow, R. S., Keller, M. B., Hoven, C. "Brief Diagnostic Interviews (SDDS-PC) for Multiple Mental Disorders in Primary Care: A Pilot Study." *Archives of Family Medicine,* 1995, *4,* 220–227.

CAROL L. ALTER, M.D., is director of the Neurosciences Division of Bristol-Meyers-Squibb and chair of the Managed Care Committee of the Academy of Psychosomatic Medicine.

PART TWO

Critical Topics at the Primary Care–Mental Health Interface

Managed care techniques first used in the private sector are increasingly being applied to control costs in the public sector. When the system places the burden of recognizing, diagnosing, and even treating mental illness on the primary care physician, however, a number of problems can result.

Gatekeeping and Authorization

Monica L. Miles, Rupert R. Goetz

Most people in the United States generally receive their medical care through an internist, a family practitioner, a pediatrician, or an obstetrician-gynecologist. There are occasionally exceptions, as for a patient with an early-onset or long-standing illness that requires specialty care who receives the bulk of this care through the specialist. For example, an insulin-dependent diabetic of juvenile onset is likely to have much of his or her care coordinated through the endocrinologist.

In much fewer cases is this true of mental illness. In certain "closed" systems, such as the military and Veterans Administration system, a young recruit may experience his first symptoms during boot camp and enter the system through psychiatry, having his health care coordinated through this point of entry. The same may apply to certain public sector systems of care for mental health where the indigent patient is seen by the psychiatrist for the psychiatric illness but, because this may be the patient's only opportunity to obtain health care, triage reveals that medical assessment and care are required. Recently, psychiatry has begun to reexamine its role as a principal physician (Wulsin, 1996) for severely and persistently mentally ill patients, including its possible role in providing physical health care (Shore, 1996).

Managing Care by Managing Access

With the move to control the costs of mental health care, the public primary care and mental health system both are increasingly turning to managed care techniques designed in the private sector for this purpose. Costs should reflect the value society places on good health (Sartorius, 1997). Controlling costs has therefore also frequently become an issue of managing (and possibly decreasing) utilization, since further discounting the price of one unit of service produces little sustained savings after a leaner pricing structure has been achieved. Thus attention shifts to how many units of service are used, with particular scrutiny placed on the most expensive services (typically "specialist" costs, such as psychiatry). This is one of the fundamental mechanisms of managed behavioral health care systems (Mihalik and Scherer, 1998). One of the most frequently employed techniques that is now also seeing increasing application in the public sector is that of "gatekeeping," imposing some type of authorization process whereby limits or conditions are placed on the services under scrutiny.

When the emerging system places the burden of recognizing, diagnosing, and even treating mental illness on the primary care physician (PCP), a number of problems can result. Psychiatric disorders may be underrecognized and may be inadequately treated, increasing morbidity for the patient. If the primary care physician is at financial risk for the mental health services to be provided, that may provide an incentive to resist referring patients. Even when referrals are made freely, a certain awkwardness is introduced into the relationship if the specialist must seek permission from a colleague before taking diagnostic or treatment steps that would have been taken automatically under the prior system. If necessary referrals are delayed, the psychiatrist may have to deal with problems that might have been more manageable with earlier appropriate intervention. Intervening at this later point may entail a number of inadvertent complications:

Correction of the original diagnosis
Institution of a change in the medication regimen
Management of treatment resistance from the patient, who may have received the subtle message that the problem is not truly a mental illness and that seeking psychiatric help is the least desirable thing to do (the hesitancy in making the referral can reinforce the stigmas that go along with having psychiatric disease)
Management of treatment resistance occurring when the patient is invested in the treatment initiated by the PCP and opposes changes
Management of resistance occurring when the patient has difficulty viewing the psychiatrist as the essential provider in treating the problem and resentment if the patient feels "passed along" rather than properly cared for

We will attempt to demonstrate through case examples the nature of the gatekeeping and authorization process and its effect on the primary care–mental health interface. Problems that arise through the application of these managed care techniques in the public sector, as well as possible solutions, are discussed.

Case 1

Mrs. Wilson, a sixty-year-old woman with no noted previous history of mental illness, begins presenting to the emergency room with chest pain, abdominal pain, and shortness of breath. She has been followed by the same primary care doctor for the past decade and has enjoyed relatively good health with the exception of hypertensive disease and smoking for twenty-five years. Her symptoms manifested approximately six months after the sudden death of her spouse of forty years, with whom she had run a family business. After multiple emergency room and office visits, Mrs. Wilson started to talk to her PCP about feeling "nervous." The PCP felt that this was related to the loss of her husband and the new responsibility of having to take care of the family business alone. He decided to start the patient on a short-acting benzodiazepine, hoping to diminish her anxiety. The patient was not happy about taking the medication but felt she needed something to help her survive. She made several attempts to stop the medication but each time experienced extreme rebound anxiety, which led to increasing the dose. She felt she was becoming addicted and did not feel that the medication improved her quality of life. Bouts of extreme anxiety between doses eventually made her unable to leave home. It was at this point a referral was made to a psychiatrist.

The psychiatric evaluation revealed a pertinent history of mood instability, anhedonia, sleep disturbance, and severe anxiety that had developed into agoraphobia. Symptoms had started two months after her husband's death. Lower-level anxiety with somatic symptoms that occurred with various stressful situations existed before the death of her husband but had not been incapacitating. Her family history showed the common use of alcohol and cigarettes, as well as heart disease and obstructive pulmonary disease. Social history revealed that the patient came from a culture where "you just dealt with your problems." The psychiatrist combined diagnosis and treatment with building trust and rapport to address the stigma of mental illness as well as education. Mrs. Wilson was given a working diagnosis of panic disorder with agoraphobia and a comorbid diagnosis of major depressive disorder. The psychiatrist first started a Selective Serotonin Reuptake Inhibitor (SSRI) to address both the anxiety and the depression. The patient was weaned off the short-acting benzodiazepine and started on a longer-acting one with the goal of avoiding the rebound anxiety, giving the SSRI a chance to gain efficacy, and then accomplishing an easier taper off the longer-acting drug.

Within four weeks the patient's symptoms had improved tremendously and her multiple visits to the ER and PCP abated. Approximately twelve weeks into treatment she was able to sell her family business, move into a new home, and obtain employment in another field. The further workup recommended by the psychiatrist revealed evidence of Chronic Obstructive Pulmonary Disease, for which the appropriate intervention was done.

This case, where the patient, a businesswoman, does not carry the hallmark of a "public" client, nevertheless illustrates an all too common pattern of interaction between primary care physician and psychiatrist. Delays in referral are inevitable when the systems are separated (for example, by gatekeeping or authorization requirements), both in the colleagues' as well as in the patient's mind. Had this patient not managed so successfully, the outcome might have been much grimmer. Earlier intervention would have reduced unnecessary suffering and decreased the expense to the general medical system of care. The nature of the psychiatric interview allowed the patient to open up with more pertinent history, which led to a diagnosis and suitable psychiatric care. This case is a good example of the first step in any gatekeeping or authorization process: the recognition of the need for the referral.

Case 2

Mr. Miller, a twenty-five-year-old man, came to his PCP after sustaining an ankle sprain from a fall. During his registration in the waiting room, the nurse noted bizarre behavior and alerted the PCP. The patient appeared "preoccupied" and when queried stated that he was concerned about "hearing and feeling the presence of people" when there was obviously no one around. He felt he was having difficulty concentrating at work or even watching TV because of it. The PCP started the patient on a high-dose sedating neuroleptic, which helped diminish the hallucinations; however, the man returned to the clinic shortly thereafter, experiencing difficult-to-tolerate side effects. He was then authorized for one visit to the psychiatrist.

Mr. Miller's psychiatric history on examination revealed a formal thought disorder with auditory hallucinations. He complained of severe sedation on the medication, causing an inability to work. He was started on a lower-dose, higher-potency neuroleptic and on a low-dose benzodiazepine.

Follow-up medication management was needed, but each subsequent visit had to be authorized individually. Although the PCP had no problem signing the authorization form, the central authorizing official felt that the patient could be followed in his primary care clinic. The treatment plan for follow-up suggested by the psychiatrist was not instituted, and the patient was left to return on an as-needed basis. This had not been communicated well to Mr. Miller, and when he tried to return to the psychiatrist, he was told that the visit had to be authorized. He and his family had understood the follow-up plan explained by the psychiatrist and sought approval for a subsequent visit. Meanwhile, Mr. Miller began to experience common side effects to the medications and called his PCP only to find the first available appointment was in five weeks. He did not want to risk the out-of-pocket expense of returning to the psychiatrist, did not call, and decided to stop his medication until he could see someone. Shortly thereafter, his psychosis returned, which led to his inability to work and suspension from his job. He was brought back to the PCP office by his family members, where he was authorized for a second visit (one only) to the psychiatrist. The medications were restarted, the side effects were determined to be manageable, and the patient improved enough to return to work after a short period. With intense family advocacy, subsequent medication management visits were approved in a more timely manner, and the patient remained stable and compliant with follow-up care.

This case, still dealing with an individual who is able to work despite a major mental illness, demonstrates how poor communication can almost lead to the patient's falling into the public system's "safety net." Should he have deteriorated more and not had an involved family to help him navigate the difficult authorization process, he might have lost his job and faced full disability. Mr. CM's psychiatric illness was blatant, and the PCP, with good intentions, attempted to address the psychosis without consultation. However, he was unable to give appropriate follow-up secondary to the barriers present in the system, which may be manageable in primary care but are inappropriate for mental health issues; the difficulty this posed to the patient experiencing a thought disorder; the "bulkiness" of the authorization process; and the busy PCP's inability to handle the psychopharmacology from the initial prescription to management of side effects. Although psychiatrists could lose some of their traditional roles in the current climate of change (Olfson, Weissman, and Gottlieb, 1997), a clear understanding of these difficulties and an offer to help despite them can go a long way toward collaborating for improved patient care.

Both cases illustrate just a small sample of the difficulties that can occur with the PCP gatekeeping and a health system authorization process on the outpatient level. Under the circumstances presented, one can easily imagine either of these cases or variations progressing to the point were inpatient treatment would be required.

The authorization process in emergencies might have been less complicated but would most likely have presented its own set of unique dilemmas. The level of acuity would have to be high to qualify as an "emergency" in most managed care systems. This may mean that using emergency authorization requires some degree of danger to self or others. Even when the threshold is met, additional problems could arise: a patient might show up at an ER that had no physicians on the particular managed care panel; a patient might destabilize "after hours," when authorization officials are not available; or a patient might be admitted but be assigned for follow-up to a different psychiatrist as an outpatient, jeopardizing continuity of care.

Where these first two cases point to common problems that will be particularly vexing and disruptive in public systems, the next will focus more on management of gatekeeping and authorization processes. In states were the complexity of these have not quite been worked out, individual psychiatrists and PCPs have come together to develop more creative solutions. Where the PCP is truly seen as the "owner" of the patient's care and the psychiatrist as the consultant, it becomes imperative for PCPs to contract in some way with mental health for their psychiatric needs. Estimates of the personnel needs to provide mental health services (Faulkner and Goldman, 1997) allow these discussions to proceed in a climate of better understanding.

Case 3

One such model in the Chicago area involves the process of grant acquisition by the primary care clinic to provide services to patients in public sector health care. The area in which this health center is located had inadequate psychiatric providers and therefore few resources to meet mental health needs. After the arrival of a practice with public sector interests, the new psychiatrist assisted in starting the process of fulfilling the mental health needs of the community. This process was slow but progressive. It began with education of the PCP doctors around recognizing mental illness and realizing when a referral to the specialist is necessary. The educational component was carried out through the mechanism of lectures attended by both residents and attending staff, grand rounds, and case conferences. Although most of this time was given pro bono by the psychiatric group, it provided the benefit of exposure to practitioners in the community who see both private and public patients. This led to setting up a funded clinic within the primary care site, where the group of psychiatrists made twice-a-month visits for a four-hour clinic preceded by lectures on common psychiatric illnesses seen in primary care. Usually the educational focus was on the things that were least recognized by the PCP. One clinic a month was led by a child and adolescent psychiatrist and the other by the two adult psychiatrists who alternated months. The practice agreed to accept a discounted fee not much different from Medicare rates, and within several months the clinic filled to capacity, double-booked at times because of the previously unrecognized need. This led to a greater number of "encounters" by the clinic, which affected the funding in a positive direction. Since the PCP remained the primary physicians, recommended laboratory tests and examinations such as electrocardiograms were considered their responsibility, and follow-up was done in subsequent psychiatric clinics for monitoring of symptoms and medications. All the while, lab tests were reviewed immediately by the PCP, who could phone the psychiatrist with any questions. Also, during psychiatric clinic times, the psychiatrist was always available between patients to answer questions and tie up loose ends. As the system developed, it was found that other areas needed development in the form of "wraparound" services (as is many times the case with the indigent mentally ill). The clinic with psychiatrist help was able to justify funding for training in psychiatric social work and consultation on this level. If therapy was determined to be in order, experience allied health professionals were available to provide it, with good supervision.

In this case, the psychiatrist and PCPs worked out a creative solution using a consultation model. It provided the PCP with the diagnostic and treatment information needed as well as follow-up in the regularly scheduled clinics. The more mundane task of prescription refills, lab orders, and follow-up were carried out by the PCP so as not to burden the psychiatrist. Since the PCPs were paid by the clinics and had access to support staff funding, their time was not an issue. There are many problems to be worked out in this setting—for example, teaching the PCPs more about DSM Axis II pathology, especially borderline and narcissistic personality disorders, as well as helping them recognize their issues of countertransference and how not to let them interfere with treatment. One other nonfunding obstacle is the lack of understanding by the PCP that a psychiatric patient is to a large extent responsible for his or her own care and that taking over for the patient is not necessarily helpful. The future looks very optimistic for this type of joint venture for both patient care and research efforts. The case illustrates how gatekeeping and authorization conflicts in this type of public system have been largely resolved through collaborative attention to financing, administration, and clinical care.

Case 4

The complexity of gatekeeping and authorization (an issue of the financial dimension on the "map" proposed in Chapter Two) is the construct of "Somatic Mental Health" under the Oregon Health Plan (OHP): Who decides what clinical care can be provided under the following circumstances? The OHP, based on a clearly integrated benefits package (described in a list of physical and mental health treatment and condition pairs) (Pollack, McFarland, George, and Angell, 1994), is still financed through two different pools: physical health is covered by the Office of Medical Assistance Programs (OMAP), and mental health is covered through the Health Plan Unit of the Mental Health and Development Disability Services Division. When actuaries began calculating rates and the funds to be placed in the risk pools, difficulties emerged. The bulk of all laboratory costs was easily attributable to primary care. However, it was understood that mental health also had laboratory costs, such as lithium levels. It was not possible to separate these cleanly, and therefore all money for laboratory costs was placed in the rate of the primary care health plans. Similar dilemmas emerged around the procedure costs for electroconvulsive therapy, since most "procedures" were performed on the physical health side. Together with difficulties in deciding whether Tegretol, for example, was being prescribed as a mood stabilizer or an antiseizure medication, a pool of money that included mental health services emerged within the primary care budget. This was labeled "Somatic Mental Health." (Funds for mental health services provided by primary care physicians were included in the primary care rate.) A great deal of discussion was required before the problem was clearly understood in both the mental and physical health communities. After all, primary care physicians were at risk to pay for laboratory tests ordered by psychiatrists. Psychiatrists were in a position where their patients could not get laboratory testing without the permission of the primary care physician, which some of the severe and persistently mentally ill patients had never been able to establish. Thus analysis of this example reveals difficulties in the dimensions of finance and clinical care at the provider, agency, and systems level.

The forum of OMAP's Medical Director Group (which had mental health input and spanned these levels) was used to arrive at a feasible resolution. A procedure was developed, under the title "Somatic Mental Health Protocol." It specified, among other things, that a psychiatrist, on seeing an OHP patient who required physical health or somatic mental health services, would inform primary care colleagues of this fact through the use of a simple one-page form that recorded basic diagnostic and treatment plan information. In turn, psychiatrists declared what a "usual and customary" amount of laboratory testing might entail in case of various major mental illnesses. Based on the fact that such a notification had occurred, laboratory costs ordered by the psychiatrist up to the quantity specified in the agreement were then automatically covered by the primary care provider. Because costs under such an arrangement could become excessive, regular review of the protocol at the medical director's group was instituted. The process, several years after its inception, has remained intact with only minor adjustments.

The development of such a process was clearly not possible without a shared understanding of the interface issues raised by the actuaries' calculation methods. The solution, which explicitly combines an examination of clinical and financial issues at the systems level and allows for broad input in clearly defined stages, appears promising. The personal relationships developed in the OMAP medical directors group fostered a climate in which decisions that supported best practice but avoided hidden financial impacts became possible.

Conclusion

Gatekeeping and authorization at the primary care–mental health interface is a classic technique that illustrates the inseparability of the financial, clinical, and administrative elements of each system. The primary care physician and the mental health provider must share an understanding of who is financially responsible for the necessary service. Only when ultimate payment responsibility is clear can smooth communication about clinical issues begin, and such understanding goes a long way toward enhancing collaboration between colleagues. After all, both are trained to serve the patient first. Nevertheless, even when a clinical consensus has been achieved, administrative issues can arise that impede the provision of services necessary for the best care of the individual patient.

One of the prerequisites for successful management of gatekeeping and authorization problems in the public sector is the financial freedom to provide flexible services. Since payment responsibility, which is shared between agencies (or even branches of government), presents its own set of barriers, it is extremely important to avoid or eradicate those arising out of the inability to approve payment for certain type of service. If both parties agree that a certain service is best provided in one setting or the other, reimbursement must follow the patient. The opportunity in dealing thoughtfully with gatekeeping and authorization in public systems lies in the ability to use these managed care techniques to advance the dialogue between primary care physician and mental health provider.

References

Faulkner, L. R., and Goldman, C. R. "Estimating Psychiatric Manpower Requirements Based on Patients' Needs." *Psychiatric Services,* 1997, *48* (5), 666–670.

Mihalik, G., and Scherer, M. "Fundamental Mechanisms of Managed Behavioral Health Care." *Journal of Health Care Financing,* 1998, *24* (3), 1–15.

Olfson, M., Weissman, M. M., and Gottlieb, J. F. "Essential Roles for Psychiatry in the Era of Managed Care." *Archives of General Psychiatry,* 1997, *54* (3), 206–208.

Pollack, D. A., McFarland, B. H., George, R. A., and Angell, R. H. "Prioritization of Mental Health Services in Oregon." *Milbank Quarterly,* 1994, 72 (3), 515–553.

Sartorius, N. "Psychiatry in the Framework of Primary Health Care: A Threat or a Boost to Psychiatry?" *American Journal of Psychiatry,* 1997, 154 (6), 67–72.

Shore, J. H. "Psychiatry at a Crossroad: Our Role in Primary Care." *American Journal of Psychiatry,* 1996, 153 (11), 1398–1403.

Wulsin, L. R. "An Agenda for Primary Care Psychiatry." *Psychosomatics,* 1996, 37 (2), 93–99.

MONICA L. MILES, M.D., is medical director of inpatient services for the Illinois Masonic Medical Center and president of Medical Behavioral Health, S.C.

RUPERT R. GOETZ, M.D., is adjunct associate professor of psychiatry and associate director of the Public Psychiatry Training Program in the Department of Psychiatry at Oregon Health Sciences University and medical director of the Office of Mental Health Services for the state of Oregon.

Collaboration is easily hampered by real or perceived differences in confidentiality that prevent two critical providers from communicating openly. However, increased communication can be a two-edged sword. Sensitive and confidential information can reach individuals who may not be directly involved in patient care.

Confidentiality

Nick Kates

In many communities, the relationship between mental health and primary care services can best be described as uneasy, often characterized by a lack of personal contact between primary care providers and by problems in communication (Craven and others, 1998; Jackson and others, 1993; Kates and others, 1987, 1992; Simon and others, 1995). Primary care providers often become frustrated when trying to refer patients for psychiatric assessment or treatment or when they hear nothing after referring a patient to a mental health service (Cassata and Kirkman Liff, 1981; Orleans, George, Houpt, and Brodie, 1985; Watters, Gannon, and Murphy, 1994). By the same token, mental health providers get concerned at the reluctance of some family physicians to play a more active role in their patients' care (Eisenberg, 1992; Lin and others, 1996).

Slowly, however, in many jurisdictions in North America, the situation is beginning to change. Although this is often a response to a specific local need, there are some common factors contributing to these changes. Initially driven by economics, collaboration between mental health and primary care providers yields numerous benefits. But collaboration can be hampered by real or perceived differences in confidentiality that prevent the two critical providers from communicating openly.

The key to success in public primary care–mental health partnerships is better communication between the providers. This can be achieved in many ways, such as rapid transmission of assessment, admission, or discharge data from mental health services to primary care providers; the provision of complete and relevant information by a primary care provider when making a referral; updates on any treatment changes; and opportunities for family physicians to discuss clinical problems with psychiatric colleagues. In recent years, transmission of data has been facilitated by advances in telecommunications (fax machines, mobile phones).

This increase in contact between professionals from different settings and disciplines, which may even involve mental health care providers working within primary care settings, can lead to a freer exchange of information.

Case Example

Mrs. Adams, a patient of Dr. Dixon, presents at a local emergency psychiatric service with symptoms of an acute episode of depression. Emergency staff decide to contact Dr. Dixon, who is able to provide relevant background information on medications (which Mrs. Adams had discontinued two weeks before) and recent work stress. During the assessment, Mrs. Adams reveals that she is involved in an extramarital affair, of which both her husband and Dr. Dixon are unaware. She requests that this information be kept confidential. Following the assessment, the emergency psychiatrist recontacts Dr. Dixon to inform him that Mrs. Adams has agreed to restart her medication and is agreeable to going home, with a follow-up appointment with Dr. Dixon scheduled for the following week. Dr. Dixon agrees to this plan. Dr. Dixon is not told about the affair, but Mrs. Adams is encouraged to raise this issue with him at their next visit.

In this example, increased communication has probably improved the comprehensiveness and continuity of care. It can, however, be a two-edged sword. A freer exchange of information can lead to a greater risk that sensitive and confidential information will reach individuals who may not be directly involved with a patient's care. Dr. Dixon works as part of a large group practice. If the Emergency Psychiatric Service were to fax the discharge summary to Dr. Dixon's office the following day, the question arises whether the practice has taken adequate steps to ensure that faxes are treated confidentially, especially if it were to allude to sensitive personal information that Mrs. Adams has requested be kept confidential. This highlights the need for great vigilance to protect this information by both the sender and the receiving facility.

Our challenge is to figure out how to ensure that greater access to information on the part of providers does not override the basic principles that data should be accessible only to individuals directly involved with a patient's care and that no data will be exchanged without the patient's knowledge and consent.

Confidentiality Issues at the Primary Care–Mental Health Interface

Because the level of protection of the confidentiality of mental health information is often greater than that provided for information in primary care, this chapter looks at these issues primarily from the viewpoint of the management of mental health information in primary care settings. Nevertheless, it is essential that communication between mental health and primary care providers be seen as a two-way street. Mental health personnel must always remember that an individual's family physician will play a central role in coordinating the patient's care and needs to be informed regularly about the patient's progress, treatment changes (especially medications), and discharge or transfer plans.

Before looking at specific steps public PCPs can take to protect patient information, it is worth reviewing some of the factors that can threaten the confidentiality of provider-patient information at the primary care–mental health interface.

Requests for Mental Health Notes in Primary Care Charts. Whatever the source of a mental health note in primary care (sent by a mental health service or provider, handwritten in the chart by a mental health worker), these notes may be as sensitive or confidential as any note in a mental health facility or psychiatrist's office and should be treated as such. They should receive the same degree of protection and the same consent before being released. Regulations in most states specify what information can be released, to whom, and for how long. A PCP's obtaining a patient's consent for the release of information, however, does not usually meet the same high standards that would be required if a mental health facility receives a request for information.

This is particularly relevant if the request comes from an insurance company or a lawyer requesting information on a client. Rarely accompanied by an official release form, such requests may demand the entire chart, which could allow the requesting parties to "trawl" through it to see what they can find. This presents a further problem, as notes can be taken and used out of context to deny a legitimate claim or to devalue the validity of other comments made by a patient. The same issue can arise with requests for information from an individual's workplace, especially if the individual has a contract with the employer that does not confer the right to refuse release of this information or if the provider is an employee or subcontractor of the requesting organization.

Content of Notes Kept in Primary Care or Sent to Primary Care Providers. Whether writing directly in a primary care chart or preparing a note to be sent to a referral source, the content of the note needs to be considered carefully. Anybody working in primary care must decide what information should be spelled out in detail in the chart, as opposed to either being alluded to or remembered but not included in a summary note.

Writing data without clarifying the context can influence further assessments, as someone taking over that person's care, either temporarily (during a vacation) or permanently, may not be quite as objective as the initial care giver. A record that describes sexual or criminal behavior that is irrelevant to the current mental health problem or states reasons for contacts with the family physician can bias an assessment in a way that may be unfair to the patient. Family physicians are often more adept than mental health providers at developing a shorthand for dealing with these issues.

Access to a Chart. Primary care providers may not be as familiar with, or even aware of, mental health confidentiality guidelines as individuals working within mental health services or hospitals. It is feasible that a new family physician who has taken over a patient's care or who is covering for a colleague may be unaware of what information has or has not been communicated to other family members. The physician may inadvertently pass on something written in a note of which a relative or the patient may have been unaware.

The risk is amplified in large group practices, where other staff (such as receptionists or secretaries) might have access to potentially sensitive data in charts, possibly relating to patients with whom they may have a social relationship, especially in a smaller community.

Caution is also required when a relative of a patient calls in to ask the receptionist if the relative has an appointment with a provider working in the practice. If the request pertained to a physical problem, the receptionist might provide this information automatically. With a visit to a mental health provider, however, disclosing any information about such a contact without explicit consent must be avoided.

Exchange of Information Between Providers. Models of improved communication often encourage discussions of a case between providers from different backgrounds or settings. This may take place in person or by phone and can be to discuss a consultation, to review a patient's progress, or to work out a plan for treatment after discharge from a mental health facility, as when the emergency room contacted Dr. Dixon after Mrs. Adams's visit. Though nothing may be written down, each provider is aware of the need to respect confidential information about a patient in the details divulged. This has to be balanced against the need to ensure that enough relevant information is transmitted to enable the other party to provide helpful advice or continue to provide effective care. In some jurisdictions, physician-to-physician contact requires no additional consent if both individuals are treating the same patient. In others, the safest approach involves obtaining consent to release information early in treatment and to inform the patient that the case may be discussed with a colleague.

New Ways of Transferring Information. The advent of newer technologies have made it much easier to transfer information between different settings. Communication between mental health and primary care services can now take place in a number of ways: by letter, fax, telephone, voice mail, e-mail, third party (such as another health provider), or directly person to person.

Many of these newer technologies, especially fax machines and telephone answering services, increase the risk that data could inadvertently be seen or received by someone not connected with the care of the individual. How, then, can confidential information being transmitted be protected?

The advent of electronic medical records, with data often being analyzed away from the primary care setting, raises new problems. If potentially sensitive information is to be transmitted, great care must be taken to determine who will have access to it and for what purposes. Data should not leave the primary care setting until some encryption has taken place, to prevent individuals from being identified. Again, the question arises of what consent patients need to provide and how much they should be told about what will happen with the data.

Patient Concerns. Patients are frequently unaware of many of these issues. They do not know how notes are kept, who has access to their record, or how information is transmitted between providers. A sometimes overlooked question that providers need to consider is how much to tell a patient about what may happen to records of sensitive issues discussed during a visit. This is a matter patients will rarely raise themselves.

Communication between providers may sometimes also be affected by a reluctance on the part of patients to allow data to be transmitted to the family physician. There may be valid reasons for this. A patient may have a personal relationship with the provider and wish to keep certain details separate from this relationship, especially in smaller communities where the choice of primary care provider may be limited or a professional relationship may inevitably have a social component.

The primary care provider may also be involved with other members of an individual's family. However much the family physician is trusted, a patient may have some concerns about information being inadvertently relayed to another family member. Patients may also worry that this information may affect the family physician's relationship with the patients themselves or with other family members.

Safeguards to Protect Confidential Information

How can we address these issues and balance the desire to enhance the quality and continuity of care an individual receives with the need to respect and maintain patient confidentiality? Although each situation needs to be examined and resolved in its own specific context, the following guiding principles are applicable in almost every situation where an issue might arise. Again, for sake of clarity, we focus primarily on recommendations that are applicable to the management of mental health data in the primary care sector. Analogous recommendations are useful in mental health settings and may even be legally required.

Sending Mental Health Records Compiled in Primary Care. To overcome the potential problems that can arise, anyone providing mental health care in primary care, irrespective of their background or discipline, should do all of the following:

1. Always inform the patient as to (a) what happens to confidential or sensitive topics that are discussed in a session in primary care, (b) any requests received for information on the patient's progress or problem, (c) what materials may be sent from a mental health service to a referral source or primary care provider, and (d) who else the provider may be talking to. Such an approach not only addresses confidentiality issues but is also consistent with the concept of seeing the patient as a partner in treatment planning.

2. Document that this discussion has taken place in the medical record.

3. Never send any mental health records compiled in a primary care setting and pertaining to a mental health issue to any third party without the appropriate consent forms' having been signed and made part of the record.

This consent should offer the highest level of protection of confidentiality (that is, it should meet the requirements of mental health legislation of that jurisdiction).

4. If an entire primary care chart has been requested without a formal release under mental health legislation, omit any notes written by a mental health professional from the materials being sent. These can be blacked out during photocopying or simply withheld. They can be sent when a formal release of information has been received.

5. Mark any materials being sent with a stamp saying "NOT TO BE COPIED."

6. Inform a patient whenever a summary or report is being sent from one provider to another.

7. If time and the situation permits, offer to allow the patient to review the final draft of a letter before it is sent to a third party. This can ensure that nothing is sent of which the patient may be unaware, which could be taken out of context, or which may be inaccurate.

8. If appropriate, send a copy of this correspondence to the patient as a record of what information is being transmitted.

9. Expectations and legal permissibility may differ from one jurisdiction to another. Although the minimum legal requirements may not always be synonymous with best clinical practices, it is necessary for providers to differentiate real (legal) issues from artificial barriers, such as clinic or hospital policies, which might stand in the way of better communication.

Content of Notes. When writing in a primary care record, mental health and primary care providers should ensure that only relevant data are included and that information is written in a manner that does not allow specific phrases or sentences to be taken or used out of context. The same applies to any letter being sent by a mental health service to a primary care provider.

Chart Access and Protection. Treat the mental health notes in a primary care chart as though the primary care setting was a mental health setting: limit access to the chart to individuals directly related to the care of that individual. All primary care staff, especially reception staff who may be unfamiliar with the criteria for mental health record confidentiality, need to be fully informed about their expectations. No one who calls a primary care setting inquiring about a relative or an acquaintance should, without the patient's consent, receive any information concerning that person's contact with a mental health care provider.

Case Discussions. Mental health and primary care providers should always consider contacting each other to discuss a case whose care they share. Confidentiality issues can be addressed by routinely informing the patient that this will happen and obtaining consent to release information that will remain on the chart. If a provider looking for assistance with the management of a case wishes to discuss a case with a colleague, this discussion should take place without the individual's name being divulged.

Patient Reluctance to Give Consent. If a patient is reluctant to give consent, this should be respected, and the patient should not be treated in a punitive way. You should discuss the patient's concerns and the reason why permission is being requested. An informed and involved patient is much more likely to agree to such a request if it is fully explained.

Using New Technologies and Electronic Communications. Great vigilance is required to ensure that there cannot be casual access to answering machines or fax machines. Even cordless or cellular phone calls cannot be considered confidential. All transmitted data should be identified as being confidential, and patients' names should not be used unless absolutely essential. The same principles apply to the use of electronic medical records and data leaving the primary care setting.

Conclusion

Increased collaboration between mental health and primary care providers can lead to better communication and greater continuity of care. This poses new problems in ensuring that patient information remains confidential. The risk is increased when mental health providers work in primary care settings, as primary care workers may not be familiar with the steps that need to be taken to protect confidential information. Provided that the patient remains an informed partner, consent is always requested, all mental health notes are treated as though they emanated from a mental health facility, and care is taken to restrict access to confidential information, these problems can be resolved, and patient care is enhanced. Comparable efforts should also be made in public mental health care systems to ensure that appropriate communication takes place. Communication needs and collaboration needs must be carefully considered. Confidentiality for particularly vulnerable patients in large public systems should not be cited as a convenient excuse for silence when best practice dictates that colleagues talk and work together.

References

Cassata, D. M., and Kirkman Liff, B. L. "Mental Health Activities of Family Physicians." *Journal of Family Practice,* 1981, *12,* 683–692.

Craven, M., Cohen, M., Campbell, D., Williams, J., and Kates, N. "Mental Health Practices of Ontario Family Physicians: A Study Using Quantitative Methodology." *Canadian Journal of Psychiatry,* 1998, *43,* 42–49.

Eisenberg, L. "Treating Depression and Anxiety in Primary Care: Closing the Gap Between Knowledge and Practice." *New England Journal of Medicine,* 1992, *326,* 1080–1083.

Jackson, G., Gater, R., Goldberg, D., Tantam, D., Loftus, L., and Taylor, H. "A New Community Mental Health Team Based in Primary Care: A Description of the Service and Its Effects on Service Use in the First Year." *British Journal of Psychiatry,* 1993, *162,* 375–384.

Kates, N., Craven, M., Webb, S., Low, J., and Perry, K. "Case Reviews in the Family Physician's Office." *Canadian Journal of Psychiatry,* 1992, *37,* 2–6.

Kates, N., Lesser, A., Dawson, D., Davine, J., and Wakefield, J. "Psychiatry and Family Medicine: The McMaster Approach." *Canadian Journal of Psychiatry*, 1987, *32*, 170–174.

Lin, E. H., Goering, P., Offord, D. R., Campbell, D., and Boyle, M.H. "The Use of Mental Health Services in Ontario: Epidemiologic Findings." *Canadian Journal of Psychiatry*, 1996, *41*, 572–577.

Orleans, C. T., George, L. K., Houpt, J. L., and Brodie, H. K. "How Primary Care Physicians Treat Psychiatric Disorders: A National Survey of Family Practitioners." *American Journal of Psychiatry*, 1985, *142*, 52–57.

Simon, G. E., Lin, E. H., Katon, W., Saunders, K., von Korff, M., Walker, E., Bush, T., and Robinson, P. "Outcomes of Inadequate Antidepressant Treatment." *Journal of General Internal Medicine*, 1995, *10*, 663–670.

Watters, L., Gannon, M., and Murphy, D. "Attitudes of General Practitioners to the Psychiatric Services." *Irish Journal of Psychological Medicine*, 1994, *11*, 44–46.

NICK KATES, M.B., B.S., F.R.C.P. (C), is associate professor in the Department of Psychiatry and Behavioral Neurosciences and associate member of the Department of Family Medicine at McMaster University; he is also director of the Hamilton-Wentworth HSO Mental Health Program.

PART THREE

Summary

Integration at the primary care–mental health interface in public systems provides the opportunity to return to values that for several decades have been pushed into the background: preventive (including rehabilitative) and population-based care.

Finding Opportunities at the Interface

Rupert R. Goetz

As we have seen, multiple opportunities and dilemmas exist when attempting to integrate care across the primary care–mental health interface. Differing systems of physical and mental health care have evolved in the public sector. Each brings its own strengths and culture. Communication across the specialties is key. Underlying this dialogue must be a working understanding of the interface itself. Each must be able to see through the other's eyes.

Effective problem solving requires that we distinguish at least three types of issues: the clinical, the administrative, and the financial. Integration along each of these three dimensions will have different consequences from viewpoint of the patient, the provider, the agency, and the system, and hence differing solutions will be required. Thoughtful analysis of integration problems against this type of "map" will help achieve an initial understanding between primary care providers and mental health providers concerning where to concentrate their efforts. Is agency reimbursement for certain services the problem? Is physician education around the appropriate treatment of depression needed? Is patient education about copayments the issue?

It will be necessary to achieve a broad consensus around this kind of "map," since what was a relationship between two physicians (each intuitively understanding the other's "medical" culture) has turned into a multipart collaboration between medical and other mental health care professionals. To paraphrase the child psychiatry maxim "Only a fool treats only the child," we might say, "Only a fool addresses only one type of issue." We might also add that we are even more the fool if each specialty is concerned about something different yet assumes that its partners are looking at the same thing.

There is much to discuss, since each view adds value to the emerging system of care. To preserve their respective strengths, particular effort is required to find effective communication strategies across the differing types of mental health and physical health practices. The holistic model of primary care meets the biopsychosocial model of mental health. A knowledge of the practice dilemmas faced by each provider type is mandatory. Similarly, both the public system and the private system bring strengths to the table; the private sector may have the technological advantage, but the public can claim the expertise of dealing with patients as a safety net. An underlying theme, however, is frequently the disruption of previously established relationships through the current evolution toward the use of managed care techniques.

Rules of integration are fluid and must be made explicit. Although a hierarchy from financial to administrative to clinical considerations might be a reality, a competing reality is doing what is best for the patient, a value on which providers of any specialty can agree. Successful integration is the key to resolution of this conflict. Without such integration, public-private partnerships will dissolve, and the emerging system, built on managed care principles, is itself at risk of dissolution. Establishment (or reestablishment) of personal contacts between providers will be crucial. Yet how can we answer the legitimate questions of system and agency administrators who must concern themselves not only with clinical care but also with the survival of their organization?

One tactical approach may be to focus on quality improvement efforts once a basic level of integration at the patient and provider level has been achieved. With the opportunities presented by the current emphasis on mental health measures (for example, by the National Commission for Quality Assurance) (Voelker, 1997), input by public mental health is likely to be welcomed. Attention should be given to its being orderly and comprehensive. The inherent distinction among structural elements (presence and authority of quality improvement systems), process elements (how these communicate), and content elements (what efforts receive attention) lends itself well to both clinical and administrative discussions; it is equally relevant to patients seeking care, to providers trying to be effective, and to agencies trying to compete for contracts. Relating costs directly to outcomes will ensure effective cost control; instead of pouring money into a medical "black hole," the payor will see exactly what is being expended on clearly identified, necessary, and integrated medical services. Money that achieves a clearly defined outcome is easy to justify, yet administrators alone will be helpless in trying to measure true outcomes of care. Can they determine which outcomes are really relevant? Patients and providers can learn to articulate their values in measurable terms. This gives them an opportunity for conceptual leadership.

Integration at the primary care–mental health interface in public systems provides an opportunity to return to values that for several decades appear to have been pushed into the background: preventive (including rehabilitation and tertiary prevention) and population-based care. If both physical and mental health outcomes are made measurable in terms we can all understand, what began as cost containment can be turned more clearly toward what is best for all individuals under our care.

The lessons that each successive wave of managed care techniques have taught us can be applied to the last frontier of public mental health service: managed care. Begun more than half a century ago as a cost control strategy in private health care, managed care has now become an opportunity to help public mental health take the next step in its evolution. As Dorothea Dix unchained the mentally ill from prisons, we are now positioned to permit our patients to return to independent meaningful lives even as the public mental health system faces bankruptcy.

Reference

Voelker, R. "Quality Standards Intend to Bring Psychiatry, Primary Care into Closer Collaboration." *Journal of the American Medical Association,* 1997, *277,* 366.

RUPERT R. GOETZ, M.D., *is adjunct associate professor of psychiatry and associate director of the Public Psychiatry Training Program in the Department of Psychiatry at Oregon Health Sciences University and medical director of the Office of Mental Health Services for the state of Oregon.*

INDEX

Back Issue/Subscription Order Form

Copy or detach and send to:
Jossey-Bass Inc., Publishers, 350 Sansome Street, San Francisco CA 94104-1342

Call or fax toll free!
Phone 888-378-2537 6AM-5PM PST; Fax 800-605-2665

Back issues: Please send me the following issues at $25 each.
(Important: please include series initials and issue number, such as MHS80.)

1.MHS_____

_____

_____

$ _____ Total for single issues

$ _____ Shipping charges (for single issues *only;* subscriptions are exempt from shipping charges): Up to $30, add $5^{50} • $30^{01}–$50, add $6^{50} $50^{01}–$75, add $7^{50} • $75^{01}–$100, add $9 • $100^{01}–$150, add $10 Over $150, call for shipping charge.

Subscriptions Please ❑ start ❑ renew my subscription to *New Directions for Mental Health Services* for the year 19___ at the following rate:

❑ Individual $63   ❑ Institutional $105
NOTE: Subscriptions are quarterly, and are for the calendar year only. Subscriptions begin with the spring issue of the year indicated above. For shipping outside the U.S., please add $25.

$ _____ Total single issues and subscriptions (CA, IN, NJ, NY and DC residents, add sales tax for single issues. NY and DC residents must include shipping charges when calculating sales tax. NY and Canadian residents only, add sales tax for subscriptions.)

❑ Payment enclosed (U.S. check or money order only)
❑ VISA, MC, AmEx, Discover Card #_____ Exp. date_____

Signature _____ Day phone _____
❑ Bill me (U.S. institutional orders only. Purchase order required.)
Purchase order #_____

Name _____
Address _____

_____

_____

Phone_____ E-mail _____

For more information about Jossey-Bass Publishers, visit our Web site at:
www.josseybass.com   **PRIORITY CODE = ND1**

OTHER TITLES AVAILABLE IN THE
NEW DIRECTIONS FOR MENTAL HEALTH SERVICES SERIES
H. Richard Lamb, Editor-in-Chief